FORTINBRAS

Prince of Norway

By Isabel K.T

* Based on characters in & with scenes from:
Hamlet, Prince of Denmark
By William Shakespeare

© Isabel K.T.

FORTINBRAS

Characters in the Play

FORTINBRAS Prince of Norway
ABELINE Princess of Norway

WESLEY Advisor to FORTINBRAS
GENERAL Friend to FORTINBRAS and GENERAL to his Army

EUSTACE Cousin to FORTINBRAS
BERGDORF Squire to EUSTACE
SERVANT TO EUSTACE
FOOL at EUSTACE'S Court

TWIN I - Adler
TWIN II - Agdar
COURT SPY - Anger
COURT SPY TWIN -Aldar

COOK
KITCHEN SERVANT

ORACLE (by mention only)
NURSE
BABY FORTI
UNCLE to FONTINBRAS

THE GHOST
HAMLET
FRANSISCO
BERNARDO
MARCELLUS
HORATIO
Ambassador to Denmark from England
A Captain in FORTINBRAS' Army

Servants, Messengers, Attendants, Soldiers, A Dog (Thyre)

© Isabel K.T.

ACT I

(Scene I)

Elsinore Castle, Denmark. An apparition crosses the stage in a blur, the lights flicker. A guard walks on stage right with a spear in hand, he turns left and right scared.

GUARD:
Halt! Who's there?

The guard turns around, he sees nothing. Then, a gust of wind flickers the lights out leaving the stage pitch black.

(Scene II)

In Norway, FORTINBRAS is in his study looking over the documents and maps that cover his desk. A regal portrait of Old King Fortinbras hangs on the wall behind him. Enters ABELINE, his wife.

© Isabel K.T.

ABELINE:
Fortinbras, I need to speak with you.

FORTINBRAS:
I'm in the middle of something dear, can it wait?

ABELINE:
Is it regarding Denmark?

FORTINBRAS:
What do you know of Denmark?

ABELINE:
I just went to see the Oracle. I come with grave news. A ghost is going to haunt us.

FORTINBRAS:
And you listen? Really.

ABELINE:
You have to listen, there is a ghost in our future, and it will cause havoc and death to all that live near it. (pause) What if it is your father?

© Isabel K.T.

FORTINBRAS:
Abbie, if it were my father why would he cause our death? Besides if it were him, I would love a chat about how he left things — after all his talk of responsibility. (Huffs) Furthermore, this tragedy has to begin with our cumulative belief in ghosts, without it the idea holds no power over us.

ABELINE:
Forti, what if you are wrong? What if there is indeed a ghost and our ignorance of it is the catalyst for this prophecy?

FORTINBRAS:
That is a fear I am prepared to deal with. The fear of losing Denmark: now, that is another story. So, excuse me, I have a meeting with my general.

ABELINE:
Does your uncle know you are doing this? I thought he told you to keep away from Denmark.

© Isabel K.T.

FORTINBRAS:
If he wishes to dangle my crown in front of Eustace, I can most certainly dangle away any recommendations that come from him.

ABELINE:
But the ghost!

FORTINBRAS:
I'll tell you what: please return to your oracle and ask for more specific details. If you can bring proof of the existence of a ghost in our proximity, then I will consider this notion of yours.

Enter Messenger.

MESSENGER:
My Lord

FORTINBRAS:
Yes, what is it?

MESSENGER:
A letter has arrived from Denmark.

© Isabel K.T.

FORTINBRAS takes the letter, the messenger leaves.

As FORTINBRAS reads the letter ABELINE looks over his shoulder.

ABELINE reads the letter out-loud in hushed tones.

THE LETTER:
"Chaos in Denmark. Whispers of Ghosts. Distraught Hamlet. Claudius King and Husband to Queen as well. Celebrations. Dark Days."

ABELINE:
What a peculiar letter.

FORTINBRAS:
It was written in haste, dear.

ABELINE:
No, I am referring to the beginning. Did you not pay attention?

FORTINBRAS:
To what exactly?

© Isabel K.T.

ABELINE:
(Points to sentence in the letter)
Whispers of ghosts.

FORTINBRAS:
Ah, yes I thought that would catch your attention. See, dear, maybe it was all about Denmark and never really about us.

ABELINE:
Of course it is about us. I don't know what it is, but that ghost is not the problem the Oracle was talking about.

FORTINBRAS:
How do you know that?

ABELINE:
Because that ghost is not related to us whatsoever. Why would my Oracle tell me of a ghost that is so far away from me? It doesn't make sense, does it?

FORTINBRAS:
Again, dear, it all depends on what you believe.

© Isabel K.T.

ABELINE:
But you believe me, right?

FORTINBRAS:
I do not not believe you.

ABELINE:
What is that supposed to mean?

FORTINBRAS:
Well, it' s not that I do not believe you. It's more like I don't believe in ghosts, nor do I wish to invite such ideas into my world.

ABELINE:
Oh please, what's the worst that could happen if you did?

FORTINBRAS:
Well, it could lead me to start questioning other beliefs I have and that would be an ideological mess at a time that requires my mind to be clear for action.

© Isabel K.T.

ABELINE:
But when has your mind ever been completely clear dear? If you can question the existence of the supernatural enough to listen to what the Oracle tells me every month then surely you must wonder on it from time to time.

FORTINBRAS:
Did it ever occur to you that I could be listening to it because it was what you did that day?

ABELINE:
Yes, yet your interest goes beyond that and we both know it.

FORTINBRAS:
Abeline, really, there is a reason I keep my military discussions separate from our home life . I cannot combine the two. I have to keep a clear decisive head to achieve things in battle. Maybe at night we can ponder on the rest of the ghost story. Right now I need to focus on what is actually happening here to create what we dream of. Poland is within our grasp and Denmark could be soon after.

© Isabel K.T.

ABELINE:
Yes, but if you don't even believe in what we talk about how are you going to make any of it work? Don't you see, if you don't pay attention to this ghost, it may be the one thing that keeps you away from success. The one thing you didn't count on.

FORTINBRAS:
Is that so? Or could it be that focusing on the ghost will undoubtedly be the end of what we want because if I give it my focus it will then distract me and make us vulnerable? (pause) If that happens, then maybe the Oracle's prophecy will come true.

ABELINE:
Fine, I see the truth in your argument. Just do me a favor and as you make your plans please keep that ghost in the periphery of your mind — just the periphery. I understand your point, however, things like this have a way of popping up when you least expect them, and apparently it can turn our world upside down... I would rather not bury my husband or find myself facing dirt thank you very much.

© Isabel K.T.

FORTINBRAS:
I will heed your warnings. Now, I have my meeting.

WESLEY, the advisor walks in. He bows.

WESLEY:
My lord, (to FORTINBRAS) my lady, (to ABELINE). We have arrived at a crossroads in our planning.

FORTINBRAS:
What do you mean, Wesley?

WESLEY:
It seems that Denmark has its own turmoil from within.

FORTINBRAS:
Expand.

WESLEY:
Well, the King is dead, Hamlet is back home but crown-less, and Claudius, late King Hamlet's brother, has taken the throne and, well, the Queen.

© Isabel K.T.

FORTINBRAS:
(Pretends to be surprised)
What is going on in Denmark?

WESLEY:
Hamlet isn't taking the news well and he is not the only one. The guards around the castle have started rumors of a ghost.

ABELINE:
A ghost!

FORTINBRAS:
A ghost? Really, where did you get all this information?

WESLEY:
We placed a spy inside the palace grounds before the last battle. The man is Nordic by birth but has lived in Denmark his whole life. I've kept correspondence with him just in case the occasion should arise where we would be in need of his services.

© Isabel K.T.

ABELINE:
You do realize the war against Denmark was lost? Why would it be a good thing to follow this man's advice?

FORTINBRAS:
That is true, but my own informant has confirmed everything Wesley is telling us.

WESLEY:
Beg your pardon my lord, your informant?

FORTINBRAS:
Come now, Wesley, what is it you always say? Two heads are better than one.

ABELINE:
It depends on the heads dear.

WESLEY:
Indeed.

FORTINBRAS:
It seems this ghost can be of use.

© Isabel K.T.

ABELINE:
Beware of the ghost; it will only cause trouble.

FORTINBRAS:
Exactly. If it is already meant to cause trouble, why not simply redirect its actions?

ABELINE:
What do you mean?

WESLEY:
What trouble?

FORTINBRAS:
Maybe the ghost is supposed to cause trouble somewhere else, not here.

ABELINE:
First, this has to mean you believe in ghosts which a minute ago you were weary about. Second, how on earth are you going to control a ghost? And last, this does not sound like a good idea.

WESLEY:
I think it's brilliant.

© Isabel K.T.

ABELINE:
Oh really? And how do you propose that my husband gets ahold of a ghost?

WESLEY:
I'll get the general at once!

FORTINBRAS:
Yes, please bring the general.

ABELINE:
What about the Oracle?

WESLEY:
What Oracle?

ABELINE:
Private matter Wesley.

WESLEY leaves reluctantly.

FORTINBRAS:
I never said it had to be a real ghost.

© Isabel K.T.

ABELINE:
Explain.

FORTINBRAS:
Well, if the people there already believe in a ghost, we will only supply them with one to haunt their castle. That way we create a distraction for when our troops arrive.

ABELINE:
You do realize that this is just what the oracle could be warning us about?

FORTINBRAS:
Anything to do with a ghost could be what the oracle is warning us about.

ABELINE:
Yes, but this morning there was no ghost.
FORTINBRAS:
Not until you mentioned it.

ABELINE:
So now my telling you could be what the warning is about?

© Isabel K.T.

FORTINBRAS:
Darling, I recommend that you stop worrying about a ghost, or return to ask for more specific details.

ABELINE:
Fine. Be careful with Wesley, he may not be a ghost but he's a coward.

FORTINBRAS:
He's my advisor dear, I am always careful, I don't want to make my father's mistakes.

ABELINE looks up at the painting behind FORTINBRAS.

ABELINE:
He would be proud of you.

FORTINBRAS:
Not yet, but once I get Denmark back and our place in Norway is secure he will be.

ABELINE:
You have the people's love.

© Isabel K.T.

FORTINBRAS:
Yes, but not their respect. I cannot rule over them just by popularity alone, not here anyway. I want to do things right. Overruling my uncle is not an option and it is not something my father would have been proud of.

ABELINE:
Overruling Hamlet's uncle is?

FORTINBRAS:
It would be fitting. Besides, (looks at the letter again) I'm not overruling him, I'm merely winning at the game he so connivingly started.

ABELINE:
I still worry.

FORTINBRAS:
I know you do, but you tend to worry.

ABELINE:
Clearly you give me the material to.

© Isabel K.T.

FORTINBRAS:
I see the truth in that, dear. I promise this campaign is the end of this.

ABELINE:
I'll go back to the oracle. Please be careful with that ghost. I wouldn't want you to join him.

FORTINBRAS:
I will.

WESLEY returns with the GENERAL.

WESLEY:
My lord, let's start planning!

ABELINE:
It's not a party, Wesley.

WESLEY:
I beg to differ, my lady.

ABELINE leaves.

© Isabel K.T.

GENERAL:
My lord

FORTINBRAS:
Has Wesley informed you of the situation?

GENERAL:
Briefly. I understand there is a ghost involved?

FORTINBRAS:
A ghost. Is that the only thing you heard? Yes, there is. Do you have the list of spies we had in Denmark during the war?

GENERAL:
Yes, two of our spies died. One has returned to Norway and the last spy is there. I believe he is the one who has kept contact with Wesley.

WESLEY:
He also has a twin brother who resides at the outskirts of Norway and tutors your cousin in Danish.

© Isabel K.T.

FORTINBRAS:
Why does Eustace want tutoring in Danish? He barely speaks Norse.

WESLEY:
That is all I know, my lord.

FORTINBRAS:
Find out more.

WESLEY:
Now?

FORTINBRAS:
Yes, now.

WESLEY leaves reluctantly. FORTINBRAS waits until WESLEY'S footsteps are out of earshot.

FORTINBRAS:
There is a ghost in Denmark, or so we hear. We will use this ghost to our advantage as a distraction. Inner turmoil leaves little time for outer battles. So, let us find the right way to take back Denmark.

© Isabel K.T.

GENERAL:
If the castle is distracted enough, then seizing it would be easier and might take a smaller army, but we would have to make sure we have that leverage.

FORTINBRAS:
I have a man on the inside already and I believe he too has a twin.

GENERAL:
(Confused)
That may not be enough.

FORTINBRAS:
That's where the twin brother may come into play. Do you remember the players we saw in Modena General ?

GENERAL:
(Catches on excitedly.)
I'm following. What are my instructions?

FORTINBRAS:
Gather and prepare the troops to leave within a fortnight. We will need a better route than the one my

© Isabel K.T.

father used, I need you to go over my markings in these charts and evaluate the best one. We must be undetected from leaving Norway until our arrival in Denmark proper, that will not come without its challenges.

GENERAL:
I'll say.

WESLEY walks in. He is disappointed at seeing the meeting has taken place without him.

FORTINBRAS:
You may leave now.

GENERAL leaves.

FORTINBRAS:
That was quick Wesley. Any news?

WESLEY:
Yes, well — your cousin wants to study in Denmark. He heard about Danish women. He figured since they are further down the map they should be warmer than Nordic ones.

© Isabel K.T.

FORTINBRAS:
Sounds like gibberish to me but knowing Eustace I bet he was hoping to marry a Danish woman of royal blood. Maybe he is unaware that the Danish Queen has re-married?

FORTINBRAS looks intently at WESLEY trying to gage a reaction.

WESLEY shrugs.

FORTINBRAS:
Never mind, my cousin' s habits are the least of my concerns at the moment. I need to meet with this twin brother you mentioned. He will need to be briefed and tested for loyalty.

WESLEY:
There is no question of loyalty your highness, he used to be part of the Danish army and one of our original spies. He returned to care for his family.

FORTINBRAS:
What does his family need?

© Isabel K.T.

WESLEY:
They are well off, I heard. Apart from being a tutor, he and his wife own a small bakery. Besides as a loyalist no further recompense may be needed than knowing he has served his country.

FORTINBRAS:
You are a loyalist as well, aren't you? Maybe no further recompense will be needed for your work this year.

WESLEY:
Well, I simply meant that it is a reward in itself to serve king — your country.

FORTINBRAS:
Oh, I see. Very well then, I want to see that his family's needs are met and that he is well taken care off. He is crucial to our operation.

WESLEY:
(Newly motivated.)
I will see to it immediately!

FORTINBRAS:
Bring him by first thing tomorrow morning.

© Isabel K.T.

(Scene III)

Dining room. ABELINE is waiting as FORTINBRAS enters the room. Dinner is served on a thick wooden table. There are two place settings next to each other, soup plates stand ready at the top.

ABELINE:
There you are.

FORTINBRAS:
Sorry, darling, we were having a discussion.

ABELINE:
About the ghost?

FORTINBRAS:
In a way, yes.

ABELINE:
Are you going to share?

FORTINBRAS:
Later. Did you see the Oracle?

© isabel K.T.

ABELINE:
I did. It's all the same: ghost-blood-tragedy.

FORTINBRAS:
I can see the ghost and blood but I cannot understand the tragedy. At least not from where I stand.

ABELINE:
That's the point. That's why I go to an Oracle. So we know what is coming our way that we may be too near-sighted to put into view.

FORTINBRAS:
The thing you are talking about, dear, is perspective, and a deeper understanding of cause and effect perhaps.

ABELINE:
No, I'm talking about intuition, premonition.

FORTINBRAS:
No one can effectively tell the future, decisions keep it in constant movement.

© Isabel K.T.

ABELINE:
What about the outcomes of battles you so proudly pronounce?

FORTINBRAS:
That is different, and as you very well saw with my father, even then it is still a gamble.

ABELINE:
Let's say the Oracle gives you pointers on your gamble.

FORTINBRAS:
Not clear ones I might add.

ABELINE:
You yourself just stated the problematics of an exactly predictable outcome.

FORTINBRAS:
Exactly. So, it would be unnecessary to worry about a prediction.

ABELINE:
Can't you use it as a guideline?

© Isabel K.T.

FORTINBRAS:
All right. I will take my strongest shield to protect me.

ABELINE:
I'm being serious.

FORTINBRAS:
As am I.

ABELINE:
We aren't going anywhere with this conversation, are we?

FORTINBRAS:
Not really. You will have to let the dead rest, my dear.

ABELINE:
Ghosts aren't technically resting darling.

FORTINBRAS:
How's your soup?

ABELINE:
Cold. Did you see your son today?

© Isabel K.T.

FORTINBRAS:
Not yet. I will go right after dinner.

ABELINE:
Fine.

(Scene IV)
Nursery. Nurse sits on a chair overlooking baby FORTINBRAS III on his cradle.
FORTINBRAS Enters. Nurse stands up and bows her head slightly.

FORTINBRAS:
Leave us.

Nurse leaves.

FORTINBRAS looks down and into the cradle.

FORTINBRAS:
How are you little one? Can't wait to speak? I don't know what you'll be so eager to say. You will reach a

© isabel K.T.

point in your life where words become obsolete, but you will need to speak to relate to others sometimes, even when words don't make sense. There is some comfort to words, you just have to be mindful of their delivery. Be honest yet tactful, be aware of who you are speaking to, who you are speaking with, and who is listening. Some people get angry when you speak the truth and others get angry when you don't. There's regret for saying things and then there's regret for not speaking up, or not speaking up in time. Regret is a dangerous thing little one. Thinking too much can make you miss an opportunity but not thinking enough can make you miss it just the same. (pause, he sighs) It's...it's... like a hunt: You have to choose the place and be sure to have on you the right weapon. After that you look carefully around you for then timing is the most crucial part of your strategy. Sometimes you are lucky enough to find someone who understands you without the need for all that. (pause, he looks at baby Fortinbras) No comment? I believe it's the first time today I don't get a question from something I've said. I should come to you more often. I hope you are enjoying the world already. Your father is going to go get us more land to play in.

© Isabel K.T.

FORTINBRAS picks up his son and kisses his baby´s head.

FORTINBRAS:
Nurse!

Nurse walks in.

NURSE:
Yes, my lord?

FORTINBRAS:
Please take the baby for a stroll in the gardens as soon as it is warm enough.

NURSE:
But my lady has advised otherwise, my lord.

FORTINBRAS:
I see. Very well then. Follow her instructions.

FORTINBRAS exits.

© Isabel K.T.

(Scene V)

FORTINBRAS walks into the bedroom. ABELINE is in a nightgown, a robe, and slippers, pacing. There is a bed, a fireplace, a table with a chess set on it, a small couch, and an empire chair.

FORTINBRAS:
Why is it that our child cannot see the sun when it is warm out?

ABELINE:
I don't want to take any risks.

FORTINBRAS:
What risks?

ABELINE:
I've been telling you all morning that something dreadful is coming.

FORTINBRAS:
Not the ghost again. Abbie, ghosts are more likely to live inside a castle than outside one.

© Isabel K.T.

ABELINE:
We don't know that! We don't know anything. It's all gibberish. Besides the Oracle said the trouble would be caused by a ghost not that the ghost would directly cause death and blood.

FORTINBRAS:
I see. So, what are we free to do?

ABELINE:
As much as it pains me to admit, I have no control over any of us to protect us. Being extra careful is all I can do, and all I can ask is that you too be extra careful with yourself because you don't listen to me.

FORTINBRAS:
That's not true. Exactly.

ABELINE:
Really? Have you actually listened to anything I said this morning?

FORTINBRAS:
I visited our son.

© Isabel K.T.

ABELINE:
Really Forti, it should be in you to see your child.

FORTINBRAS:
But it isn't. It's not like my father spent his days in my nursery, or like I enjoy having a conversation about dead people every time I see my wife, but it seems important to you so I do it.

ABELINE:
You know what really is important to me?

FORTINBRAS:
What?

ABELINE:
Our lives. By "our" I mean, yours, mine, and our child's. Why else do you think I consult an Oracle every week? Your father had brilliant military strategists, apothecaries, and physicians; he possessed great power, but nothing could save his life or your mother's. I don't want that for us.

FORTINBRAS:
Abbie everyone must die at some point.

© Isabel K.T.

ABELINE:
I know that, don't you think I know that? I just would prefer it would be later –much much later- rather than sooner.

FORTINBRAS embraces ABELINE.

FORTINBRAS:
I understand darling. I want that too. I want to make my father proud but I also want to procure my future with you and our son. If I don't get that piece of Denmark I don't know what will happen when my uncle dies. What if my cousin gets the throne? I don't want to start a war in my own country, but I do not trust him to leave us alone.

ABELINE:
Why can't he leave us alone?

FORTINBRAS:
He is very insecure, he will only see me as a threat to his power, as I am sure his advisors will guarantee. It would only be a matter of time before he created conflict for us. Maybe then the ghost would be the least of our problems.

© Isabel K.T.

ABELINE:
Don't laugh, what if it is listening to us right now?

FORTINBRAS:
Who? The ghost?

ABELINE:
No, your cousin. Of course the ghost!

FORTINBRAS:
Well then, we could only guarantee the ghost that we are good people that don't seek to hurt it and maybe if it is listening to us it will tell us what it wants, and that way we can help him cross over.

ABELINE:
You know an awful lot about ghosts for someone who doesn't believe in them.

FORTINBRAS:
I did have a very imaginative childhood dear. See, you have nothing to worry about, if it were here it would have taken the opportunity to show itself.

© Isabel K.T.

ABELINE:
What if the ghost really is in Denmark? What then?

FORTINBRAS:
Well if it is in Denmark then it is too far away.

ABELINE:
No, but you are focusing all your time on this Danish ghost story. What if that really is it?

FORTINBRAS:
Allow me a small suggestion. What if, we live our lives in peace and keep an eye out for a ghost? That way the ghost doesn't suck the life right out of us before his tragedy strikes.

ABELINE:
I have been a little intense haven't I?

FORTINBRAS:
Only a little. If it helps, we can warn the rest of the guards to be on the lookout for suspicious movements. We don't have to explain about a ghost; we'll just tell them to be on the look-out for the symptoms of one.

© Isabel K.T.

ABELINE:
It's not a disease.

FORTINBRAS:
It's starting to feel like one.

ABELINE:
Alright. That sounds like a good plan to me. Maybe we can have a picnic and take the little one with us to get some fresh air when it's warmer out.

FORTINBRAS:
That sounds like a good plan to me.

ABELINE:
Are you coming to bed now?

FORTINBRAS:
Darling, I'd love to, but I still have to work out some details with my general.

ABELINE:
Can't it wait until tomorrow? I really don't want to sleep alone right now.

© Isabel K.T.

FORTINBRAS:
Let me go back and tell him what else we need figured out. If you can wait, I will be back.

ABELINE:
I'll wait.

FORTINBRAS:
Good.

FORTINBRAS kisses ABELINE and leaves.

ABELINE:
If only I could find a way out of all this mess. (She looks up and around.)
Please help me, whatever you are out there. Help me understand what my husband is going through so I can help him. If you are a ghost, would you mind terribly appearing so we could chat? Perhaps I can help you with what you want and with that you could be free. I have money. I could give a message to a loved one? What is it that someone like you would need to stay back for? Who are you may be a better question start with. Maybe you are not even here and I am talking pure nonsense. Maybe you really are in

© Isabel K.T.

Denmark. I just wish I could get some answers. ABELINE calm yourself you sounds like a mad woman.

ABELINE takes a deep breath and sits down on the chair by the fire. She quickly falls asleep.

(Scene VI)

FORTINBRAS walks into his study. Sits on his chair and waits for the GENERAL.

GENERAL walks in.

GENERAL:
I have reviewed all the charts and sent word to Adler and his twin in Denmark to start as planned (He places the charts on the desk). There is an alternate route here, it will take longer and is more complicated to travel but it will also ensure safe and disguised passage for all our troops for the longest time.

FORTINBRAS:
How many days are we looking at?

© Isabel K.T.

GENERAL:
If we follow it all the way to here, the boarders of Denmark, around a month. This does mean that once we reach the borders here, we will be spotted. Which gives us a couple of days' time to reach the palace. Or at least to reach the area where we will find some resistance.

FORTINBRAS:
Can we manage their resistance with the number of troops we are planning to take?

GENERAL:
It should be an even fight; however, if we do maintain the element of er 'surprise' all the way, the odds will be in our favor. If you agree, I'll message Adler in the morning.

FORTINBRAS:
Not Adler. Agner. Agner is twin to Aldar, Agdar is ting to Adler.

GENERAL:
We couldn't find a less confusing pair of twins my Lord?

© Isabel K.T.

FORTINBRAS:
Apparently not.

GENERAL:
So, Agner will meet Aldar in this opening here, and meanwhile Adler and Agdar will be invisible to all except as ghosts?

FORTINBRAS:
Exactly! Once we reach this point here (pointing at the map) our twin Agner will head on his own to meet his brother Aldar, that would-be Wesley's spy. He, Aldar, will provide him, his brother Agner, with a uniform and together they will ensure our entrance through this area over here. Now, if our first element of surprise works then we may not even need this entrance, their troops will not be active and I am sure their monarchs ´ thoughts will be otherwise engaged.

GENERAL:
That is a big "if "my lord.

FORTINBRAS:
Perhaps, but you have no idea what a silly ghost can do to a man's mind. My whole day has been thrown

© Isabel K.T.

upside down by the discussion of wether it can or cannot exist. Imagine having an actual “ghost” creating havoc in your home.

GENERAL:
I’m sorry my lord, but are we talking about real ghosts now?

FORTINBRAS:
The mere idea of one has caused enough chaos in my day, imagine if one actually spoke to people and told stories about what it saw happen when no one was looking. I say, it could drive you mad!

GENERAL:
Maybe not mad, but very distracted certainly.

FORTINBRAS:
Yes, mad to distraction! Insanity must certainly be aligned with other causes. I would think at the very least a great deal of emotion would have to be placed on the subject to truly affect you. Otherwise it will just frustrate or terrify you out of focus.

© Isabel K.T.

GENERAL:
Which is exactly what we are looking for?

FORTINBRAS:
Exactly. I am expecting the Nordic twin, Agner, tomorrow morning. Please brief him as he comes in on the military tactics of the operation. I am sure Wesley will have mentioned things in passing.

GENERAL:
I will, sir.

FORTINBRAS:
Good. That is all for now. I will see you tomorrow.

GENERAL exits one way, FORTINBRAS leaves the other.

(Scene VII)

FORTINBRAS and ABELINEs bedroom. FORTINBRAS returns to the room to see ABELINE on the chair having fallen asleep. He goes to her.

© Isabel K.T.

FORTINBRAS:
Darling?

ABELINE:
Hmm

FORTINBRAS:
Can you walk?

ABELINE:
You are back?
FORTINBRAS:
Yes.

ABELINE:
Good.

FORTINBRAS laughs. He picks her up and puts her on the bed. He takes her slippers off.

FORTINBRAS:
Good night.

ABELINE:
Good night.

© Isabel K.T.

FORTINBRAS kisses her cheek. He goes to the chair by the fireplace and sits to ponder.

ABELINE suddenly sits up in a fright.

ABELINE:
NO! (breathing raggedly) Forti are you here?

FORTINBRAS rushes to her side.

FORTINBRAS:
Abbie, I'm here what's wrong?

ABELINE:
You are here!

FORTINBRAS:
Yes, what is going on?

ABELINE:
I just had the most awful nightmare!

FORTINBRAS:
Shh, darling, it was only that.

© Isabel K.T.

ABELINE:
I don't know.

FORTINBRAS:
Let me guess, there was a ghost?

ABELINE:
No, really Forti it was too vivid.

FORTINBRAS:
What was it?

ABELINE:
You were visiting a grave, and you were really sad.

FORTINBRAS:
Could you see the name on the grave? Maybe it was just your memory of my father's burial.

ABELINE:
No, it wasn't that. The place was different. I don't know how to explain it, but you were so sad and worried.

© isabel K.T.

FORTINBRAS:
I'm here, and it's all right.

ABELINE:
But what if it is true?

FORTINBRAS:
Abbie you have to let these things go. We don't know if they are true or not right now, but you can't keep letting them dictate your life. Let's take each day at a time and just keep our eyes open. Alright darling? I promise you I will be careful but that is all we can really do.

ABELINE:
I could go back to my Oracle...

FORTINBRAS:
Abbie your Oracle will always give you open answers because the future cannot be set in stone.

ABELINE:
Fine. When did you become so wise?

© Isabel K.T.

FORTINBRAS:
When I married you.

ABELINE:
Wiser every second. Alright, promise me you will be careful?

FORTINBRAS:
It's already a promise, and you know me to be a man of my word. Now, please go to sleep. We will figure out tomorrow when it comes.

ABELINE:
What if-

FORTINBRAS:
Abbie, tomorrow will come, let's just get some rest so we can be ready for it. I'll stay right here next to you.

FORTINBRAS gets on the bed and hugs her. He blows out the candle. Stage fades to black.

ABELINE:
Fine.

© Isabel K.T.

ACT II

(Scene I)

Back at Elsinore Castle. The Twins (ADLER and AGDER) get ready to scare the guards. We see them putting on the same costume and preparing a contraption that will add the "glowing" effect and the ghostly brume.

(Scene II)

Elsinore, platform before the castle. HORATIO comes to see the ghost.

Francisco at his post. Enter to him BERNARDO.

BERNARDO:
Who's there?

FRANCISCO:
Nay, answer me: stand, and unfold yourself.

© Isabel K.T.

BERNARDO:
Long live the king!

FRANCISCO:
Bernardo?

BERNARDO:
He.

FRANCISCO:
You come most carefully upon your hour.

BERNARDO:
'Tis now struck twelve. Get thee to bed, Francisco.

FRANCISCO:
For this relief, much thanks. 'Tis bitter cold, And I am sick at heart.

BERNARDO:
Have you had quiet guard?

FRANCISCO:
Not a mouse stirring.

© Isabel K.T.

BERNARDO:
Well, good night.
If you do meet Horatio and Marcellus,
The rivals of my watch, bid them make haste.

FRANCISCO:
I think I hear them — Stand! Who's there?

Enter Horatio and Marcellus.

HORATIO:
Friends to this ground.

MARCELLUS:
And liegemen to the Dane.

FRANCISCO:
Give you good night.

MARCELLUS:
O, farewell, honest soldier. Who hath relieved you?

FRANCISCO:
Bernardo has my place. Give you good night.

© Isabel K.T.

Exit

MARCELLUS:
Holla! Bernardo!

BERNARDO:
Say—what, is Horatio there?

HORATIO:
A piece of him.

BERNARDO:
Welcome, Horatio. Welcome, good Marcellus.

MARCELLUS:
What, has this thing appear'd again to-night?

BERNARDO:
I have seen nothing.

MARCELLUS:
Horatio says 'tis but our fantasy,
And will not let belief take hold of him
Touching this dreaded sight, twice seen of us.
Therefore, I have entreated him along

© Isabel K.T.

With us to watch the minutes of this night,
that if again this apparition come,
He may approve our eyes and speak to it.

HORATIO:
Tush, tush, 'twill not appear.

BERNARDO:
Sit down awhile,
And let us once again assail your ears,
That are so fortified against our story,
What we have two nights seen.

HORATIO:
Well, sit we down, and let us hear Bernardo speak of this.

BERNARDO:
Last night of all,
When yond same star that's westward from the pole
Had made his course to illume that part of heaven
Where now it burns, Marcellus and myself,
the bell then beating one—

Enter Ghost.

© Isabel K.T.

MARCELLUS:
Peace, break thee off; look, where it comes again!

BERNARDO:
In the same figure, like the king that's dead.

MARCELLUS:
[to HORATIO] Thou art a scholar— speak to it, Horatio.

BERNARDO:
Looks it not like the king? —Mark it, Horatio.

HORATIO:
Most like. It harrows me with fear and wonder.

BERNARDO:
It would be spoke to.

MARCELLUS:
Question it, Horatio.

HORATIO:
[To the GHOST]
What art thou that usurp'st this time of night,
Together with that fair and warlike form

© Isabel K.T.

In which the majesty of buried Denmark
Did sometimes march? by heaven I charge thee, speak!

MARCELLUS:
It is offended.

BERNARDO:
See, it stalks away!

HORATIO:
[to the GHOST] Stay! speak, speak! I charge thee, speak!

Exit Ghost.

MARCELLUS:
'Tis gone, and will not answer.

BERNARDO:
How now, Horatio! you tremble and look pale.
Is not this something more than fantasy?
What think you on't?

HORATIO:
Before my God, I might not this believe

© Isabel K.T.

Without the sensible and true avouch
Of mine own eyes.

MARCELLUS:
Is it not like the king?

HORATIO:
As thou art to thyself.
Such was the very armour he had on
When he the ambitious Norway combated.
So frown'd he once, when, in an angry parley
He smote the sledded Polacks on the ice.
'Tis strange.

MARCELLUS:
Thus twice before, and jump at this dead hour,
With martial stalk hath he gone by our watch.

HORATIO:
In what particular thought to work I know not.
But in the gross and scope of my opinion
This bodes some strange eruption to our state.

MARCELLUS:
Good now, sit down, and tell me, he that knows,

© Isabel K.T.

Why this same strict and most observant watch
So nightly toils the subject of the land
And why such daily cast of brazen cannon,
And foreign mart for implements of war,
Why such impress of shipwrights, whose sore task
Does not divide the Sunday from the week:
What might be toward, that this sweaty haste
Doth make the night joint-labourer with the day,
Who is't that can inform me?

HORATIO:
That can I—
At least, the whisper goes so: our last king,
Whose image even but now appear'd to us,
Was, as you know, by Fortinbras of Norway,
Thereto prick'd on by a most emulate pride,
Dared to the combat; in which our valiant Hamlet—
For so this side of our known world esteem'd him—
Did slay this Fortinbras, who by a seal'd compact
Well ratified by law and heraldry,
Did forfeit, with his life, all those his lands
Which he stood seized on to the conqueror;
Against the which, a moiety competent
Was gaged by our King; which had return'd
To the inheritance of Fortinbras,

© Isabel K.T.

Had he been vanquisher; as, by the same covenant,
And carriage of the article design'd
His fell to Hamlet. Now, sir, young Fortinbras,
Of unimproved mettle hot and full,
Hath in the skirts of Norway here and there
Shark'd up a list of lawless resolutes,
For food and diet, to some enterprise
That hath a stomach in't, which is no other—
And it doth well appear unto our state—
But to recover of us, by strong hand
And terms compulsative those foresaid lands
So by his father lost. And this, I take it,
Is the main motive of our preparations.
The source of this our watch, and the chief head
Of this post-haste and romage in the land.

BERNARDO:
I think it be no other but e'en so.
Well may it sort that this portentous figure
Comes armed through our watch so like the king
That was and is the question of these wars.

HORATIO:
A mote it is to trouble the mind's eye.
In the most high and palmy state of Rome,

© Isabel K.T.

A little ere the mightiest Julius fell,
The graves stood tenantless and the sheeted dead
Did squeak and gibber in the Roman streets
As stars with trains of fire, and dews of blood,
Disasters in the sun; and the moist star
Upon whose influence Neptune's empire stands,
Was sick almost to doomsday with eclipse.
And even the like precurse of fierce events,
As harbingers preceding still the fates,
And prologue to the omen coming on,
Have heaven and earth together demonstrated
Unto our climature and countrymen.

Enter ADLER as Ghost from a different side, we can see the twin on the opposite side looking at the action on stage trying not to laugh.

But soft, behold— lo, where it comes again!
I'll cross it, though it blast me.
Stay, illusion!

ADLER as Ghost spreads his arms

If thou hast any sound, or use of voice,
Speak to me.

© Isabel K.T.

If there be any good thing to be done,
that may to thee do ease and grace to me,
Speak to me.
If thou art privy to thy country's fate,
Which, happily, foreknowing may avoid,
O, speak!
Or if thou hast uphoarded in thy life
Extorted treasure in the womb of earth—
For which, they say, you spirits oft walk in death—

AGDAR makes the sound of a cock crowing.

Speak of it: stay, and speak! —Stop it, Marcellus.

ADLER as Ghost exits.

MARCELLUS:
Shall I strike at it with my partisan?

HORATIO:
Do, if it will not stand.

They look around looking to find the ghost.
This time AGDAR as Ghost appears from the opposite side. BERNARDO sees him.

© Isabel K.T.

BERNARDO:
'Tis here!

AGDAR as Ghost crosses the stage and disappears onto the back.

Then ADLER as Ghost appears again from the side in which it was before.

HORATIO:
'Tis here!

Exit ADLER as Ghost disappearing in the brume.

MARCELLUS:
'Tis gone!

MARCELLUS:
We do it wrong, being so majestical,
To offer it the show of violence,
For it is, as the air, invulnerable,
And our vain blows malicious mockery.

BERNARDO:
It was about to speak, when the cock crew.

© Isabel K.T.

To the side we see the twins together looking on and trying not to laugh as they see MARCELLUS, BERNARDO, and HORATIO trying to make sense of what they just saw.

HORATIO:
And then it started like a guilty thing
Upon a fearful summons. I have heard
The cock, that is the trumpet to the morn,
Doth with his lofty and shrill-sounding throat
Awake the god of day, and, at his warning,
Whether in sea or fire, in earth or air,
Th'extravagant and erring spirit hies
To his confine; and of the truth herein
This present object made probation.

MARCELLUS:
It faded on the crowing of the cock.
Some say that ever 'gainst that season comes
Wherein our Saviour's birth is celebrated,
The bird of dawning singeth all night long;
And then, they say, no spirit dares stir abroad;
The nights are wholesome; then no planets strike,
No fairy takes, nor witch hath power to charm,
So hallow'd and so gracious is the time.

© Isabel K.T.

HORATIO:
So have I heard and do in part believe it.
But, look, the morn, in russet mantle clad,
Walks o'er the dew of yon high eastward hill.
Break we our watch up, and by my advice,
Let us impart what we have seen to-night
Unto young Hamlet; for, upon my life,
This spirit, dumb to us, will speak to him.
Do you consent we shall acquaint him with it,
As needful in our loves, fitting our duty?

MARCELLUS:
Let's do't, I pray; and I this morning know
Where we shall find him most conveniently.

Exeunt

The twins are taking off their costumes when a gust of wind appears out of nowhere and puts out their candles.

The stage goes black.

© Isabel K.T.

(Scene III)
FORTINBRAS' study, early morning.
GENERAL arrives, WESLEY is already there.

WESLEY:
What are you doing here?

GENERAL:
I was called. What are you doing here?

WESLEY:
I have a letter.

He waves it in front of the GENERAL.

GENERAL:
That letter has been opened.

WESLEY:
Well yes, I am the royal advisor.

© Isabel K.T.

GENERAL:
Even if that argument were enough it's a matter of personal privacy don't you think?

WESLEY:
His father didn't keep anything from me therefore he shouldn't either.

GENERAL:
That is his choice.

WESLEY:
What do you make of this ghost story?

GENERAL:
Was the letter about that?
WESLEY:
Perhaps.

GENERAL:
You can read the royal mail but cannot answer questions straightforwardly regarding its content?

© Isabel K.T.

WESLEY:
Perhaps it is not clear General that our roles in this castle are very different.

GENERAL:
Perhaps you are right. I shouldn't be discussing ghosts with you if you haven't been informed of the situation yourself.

WESLEY:
Or perhaps I am merely trying to see how much it is you really know.

GENERAL:
Perhaps.

FORTINBRAS walks in.

FORTINBRAS:
Good morning, General. Wesley, would you mind summarizing the contents of the letter.

WESLEY:
I beg your—?

© Isabel K.T.

FORTINBRAS:
Please Wesley, I grew up around my father, did you think I didn't know about your curiosity with the royal mail? Come on what does it say?

WESLEY:
Well, it just states that our spy is starting to believe in the existence of an actual ghost.

FORTINBRAS:
How is that relevant?

GENERAL:
I don't see this being a problem with our plan my lord.

FORTINBRAS:
Last night I had a revelation. It came to me in a dream. Strange really, but having heard this letter it makes even more sense that we proceed this way. Wesley I need you to answer our spy and tell him to keep close watch on Hamlet. Even if he has to fight with the other servants to bring him supper or a glass of water; have him do it. Once the letter is sent, come back in here.

© Isabel K.T.

WESLEY tries not to show his annoyance at being ordered out of the room yet again.

WESLEY:
Isn't there anything else I can assist with my lord?

FORTINBRAS:
Not really. Thank you for asking.

WESLEY bows and leaves.

GENERAL:
My lord, I understand I am not your advisor but as an old friend, are you not bothered by the...hmm...letter situation?

FORTINBRAS:
I appreciate your concern General but my private matters are not delivered through the royal mail. Now, let's get to business.

GENERAL:
You mentioned a dream?

© Isabel K.T.

FORTINBRAS:
Yes, in my dream I myself was a ghost. Very interesting really, I could fly freely over and through any area of the castle. It allowed me a panoramic perspective of sorts. We have chaos in the Danish court, however right now there are more pressing matters here. In the dream I left for Denmark, but while I was there, someone else was here taking my lands. Then I woke up and went to look at the books. Looking over the latest records on the books I saw a sudden decline in crop numbers. There are some things I need to settle here first before we move on with the trip to Poland and Denmark.

GENERAL:
My lord?

FORTINBRAS:
Has there been any military movement in the East of Norway?

GENERAL:
No, my lord.

© Isabel K.T.

FORTINBRAS:
Any reason to suspect there might be?

GENERAL:
None that I can think of at the moment.

FORTINBRAS:
Interesting. I need you to assign a small guard to keep an eye out for movement within Nordic borders while you to start preparing the troops and continue correspondence with our twins in Denmark. I want to know everything that they see.

GENERAL:
Yes, my lord.

FORTINBRAS:
Have you heard from Adler? Aldar? Our twin here in Norway?

GENERAL:
Yes, he has contacted his brother. He is ready to leave on a moment's notice. Wesley has briefed him as well.

© Isabel K.T.

FORTINBRAS:
And what do you know of our Danish A's?

GENERAL:
Everything is going according to plan. Even Agdar is starting to believe the existence of a ghost.

FORTINBRAS:
Isn't that what Wesley just mentioned?

GENERAL:
I believe he was referring to Agner, Aldar's twin. Which must mean that the people around Elisnore are believing more and more in this Ghost.

FORTINBRAS:
Excellent! So now Agdar is starting to believe in a Ghost?

GENERAL:
That's correct. He mentioned strange things keep happening.

© Isabel K.T.

FORTINBRAS:
I wonder if it is his own mind playing tricks on him. He is after all pretending to be one.

GENERAL:
That could be. Poor fellow.

FORTINBRAS:
Yes. Good thing this is temporary.

GENERAL:
Is there anything else you wish to go through my lord?

FORTINBRAS:
Not at the moment. General, needless to say this conversation and all that transpires with our ghostly twins is strictly between us.

GENERAL:
Yes sir.

GENERAL bows and leaves.

© Isabel K.T.

(Scene V)

A few miles East at Eustace's Castle...

EUSTACE is eating in his study when WESLEY comes in.

WESLEY:
My lord.

EUSTACE:
Yes, Wesley come in. Do you have any news?

WESLEY:
None my lord. There came a message from Denmark but the content was of little consequence.

EUSTACE:
What was the content Wesley?

WESLEY:
The spy just spoke about his personal concerns for the existence of a ghost in the castle.

EUSTACE:
What is it with these people and ghosts?

© Isabel K.T.

WESLEY:
I do not know my lord.

EUSTACE:
Very well then, anything else?

WESLEY:
The plan to march on Denmark continues. The General was at the meeting as well.

EUSTACE:
Oh.

WESLEY:
He had nothing to share he is a very private man my lord.

EUSTACE:
He knows more than you do Wesley, we need to get to him. Do we know any weakness he might have? Desires we may fulfill?

WESLEY:
None that I am aware of. I have looked for the last month.

© Isabel K.T.

EUSTACE:
How about an ambition?

WESLEY:
His ambitions seem to be fulfilled by Fortinbras.

EUSTACE:
Now, that cannot do. There has to be something out there to move his feet in our direction. After all, the best kingdom needs the best General, and I won't let my cousin near that throne.

WESLEY:
I think your cousin is after the Danish throne my lord, not your Uncle's.

EUSTACE:
I don't believe his desire for one kingdom to be exclusive of the other.

WESLEY:
What would you like me to do?

© Isabel K.T.

EUSTACE:
Keep me informed of everything, and keep a very close eye on the General. I want to know how he lives his days, what he likes, what he dislikes, anything and everything about the man that can give us a clue as to what we can offer.

WESLEY:
Yes, my lord.

EUSTACE:
You can go now Wesley, come back when you have useful information for me.

WESLEY bows and exits.

EUSTACE:
Claps his hands and a servant walks in.

Enter Servant.

SERVANT:
My lord?

© isabel K.T.

EUSTACE:
The wine is warm, change it.

SERVANT:
Yes my lord.

EUSTACE:
—and call Bergdorf. Tell him I need him.

Servant takes away the goblet at the table and walks away.

EUSTACE grabs a piece of chicken and starts gnawing at it.

EUSTACE:
(to himself, as he chews)
What does Fortinbras want with a ghost? Really, what these people believe now-a-days. On the other hand, it could be quite beneficial that he is so distracted. While he plans for Denmark I will plan for Norway. Uncle doesn't have much time left. Even then, perhaps I can get the crown from him before he goes. He is weak enough. No doubt noble Fortinbras would get in the way and with that General my hard work could

© Isabel K.T.

becomes useless. I need that General, or to get Fortinbras on his weak heel. But what is it? He didn't show fear in childhood, wasn't someone that was pushed around or who pushed others. Always giving orders but that doesn't say anything, his father was a military man. He is a bit hot headed but not enough, less so with Abeline at his side. A, my uncle had a weakness, he was too trusting of his advisors, too eager to prove, but Fortinbras noticed that too. Now I'm stuck with Wesley, whose loyalty I can't be sure of, while Fortinbras doesn't even tell him the information I need and with the slightest of incentives Wesley could let slip my plans. No, I have to make sure Wesley stays loyal to me, finds a weakness for Fortinbras, and a selling point for the General. So much to do, so little time. I need a distraction.... Where is that fool? Bergdorf!

Enter BERGDORF.

BERGDORF:
Yes, my lord?

EUSTACE:
Where is the fool?

© Isabel K.T.

BERGDORF:
He is eating my lord.

EUSTACE:
Get him here now.

BERGDORF:
As you wish, my lord.

BERGDORF leaves.

EUSTACE:
Next, find me a wife and once I get Norway why not align with Denmark? Hmm, perhaps I could advise Hamlet of Fortinbras' plans for Denmark. No, Claudius, he is the one to tell. Make friend's with my enemy's enemy? Not so sure that would work, it brings Denmark and Norway closer than comfortable. I may not be a loyal family member but a loyal Nordic is another story, that or is it perhaps loyal to power. Ahh, that must be it. The rush, the thirst, the thrill of getting it and the anguish of having it so close and so far away. I can't even remember when it all started but once you've tasted it and let it's sweet taste take over, you cannot walk away from the opportunity of more.

© Isabel K.T.

You cannot enjoy any other taste the same. Who would? Why would someone even try? It's hopeless to resist the temptation. Nothing else seems important in comparison. There is only one thing I need to focus on and that is my crown. Killing Fortinbras? The last option but an option nevertheless. Hmm, I wonder if his own death bothers him? Perhaps knowing his life is in danger would be enough of an incentive for him to back off? No, Fortinbras is much to courageous for that. Perhaps if the life of someone he loves is in danger.... Just perhaps...Does he even believe in love? He is a noble soul, noble souls always do don't they? Always fall for the softness of it. Something to be noble for... perhaps the bread is there. Wesley should be back soon. I can just ask and Wesley will deliver. But what to ask? What to ask? That is the question!

BERGDROF enters.

BERGDORF:
My lord.

EUSTACE:
Yes.

© Isabel K.T.

BERGDORF:
The fool.

EUSTACE:
Yes.

BERGDORF:
He is here.

EUSTACE:
Make him wait, bring me ink and paper and send for a messenger at once.

BERGDORF:
Yes, my lord.

EUSTACE continues to eat and chew loudly when BERGDORF rushes back in with ink and paper. He cleans an area of the table to place them on top. EUSTACE grabs the ink and starts writing, BERGDORF waits by the side patiently in silence.

After a moment EUSTACE finishes; he grabs a candle from the table and seals the letter with wax dripping, stamping the wax with his ring.

© Isabel K.T.

EUSTACE:
Where is that messenger?

BERGDORF:
Right away.

BERGDORF exits just to bring in the Messenger with him moments later.

MESSENGER:
You wanted to see me my lord?

EUSTACE:
Take this to the King of Denmark and get back here at once. I will know if you did not do as you are told.

Messenger gulps scared.

MESSENGER:
O-Of course my lord.

Messenger exits.

© isabel K.T.

EUSTACE:
Let´s see how you get out of this one Fortinbras. Bergdorf, let the fool in.

BERGDORF brings the FOOL in.

FOOL:
You called my lord?

EUSTACE:
Indeed.

FOOL:
What would satisfy your thirst today?

EUSTACE:
Only Norway.

FOOL:
I hear the sea is bountiful my lord, and it seems to like Norway enough to share itself with its shores. After all, it hugs its corners and remains a faithful companion throughout time. (pause) Would you like a drink of salt?

© Isabel K.T.

EUSTACE:
Of salt fool?

FOOL:
Yes salt, if the sea is full of salt and your thirst can only be quenched with Norway, then the salt in the sea that washes on our shores would then too run through your veins and quench that thirst. It is also easier.

EUSTACE:
Easier fool?

FOOL:
Easier to carry, easier to spread around, easier guarantee preservation.

EUSTACE:
Salt does not quench thirst fool.

FOOL
It depends on the thirst my lord. It also comes with blessings. It enriches what it touches, bringing out the best to savor, and as it preserves it opens the

© Isabel K.T.

possibility of time. What to do with it? Well that is another matter.

EUSTACE:
I know what to do with time fool.

FOOL:
Of course. Salt, like time, is delicately strong. If you know how to use it, it will enrich where you spread it, bringing out the best of what absolves it. To do this wisely you must first know your own mind, for if you just spread the salt excitedly about without council or thought then everything will be monotonous or dry, left with little space for change or the flourishing of — well anything. Now, if you spread reservedly in fear, then it may be better not to spread it at all, for it will only be done in waste. Either way, it's all in salt!

EUSTACE:
Salt is interesting. You speak truth fool.

FOOL:
That is the only thing I know how to do.

© Isabel K.T.

EUSTACE:
I find that hard to believe.

FOOL:
Sometimes it is harder to believe the truth in the mouth of a fool than the lies of the seemingly honest man, but the fool is not at fault, the truth was merely placed in his mouth, to some it amuses to others it bemuses.

EUSTACE:
What nonsense! Next you'll be talking about ghosts!
FOOL:
Not for another couple of months, perhaps. Although I hear they are in fashion.

EUSTACE:
Where do you hear that?

FOOL:
A cousin's cousin keeps writing complains from Denmark. Saying a ghost may be on the loose because strange things keep happening.

© Isabel K.T.

EUSTACE:
I wouldn't put it past the Danish to believe in ghosts, but we are not the Danes.

FOOL:
We are all humans.

EUSTACE:
Meaning.

FOOL:
Dane or Nordic, fear affects humans alike.

EUSTACE:
But the type of fear changes with knowledge and that is where we differ. How little you know! Then again you are a fool.

FOOL:
Perhaps, but the reception of it does not change, whatever the fear the reaction it causes in the body is the same. How we grow the fear in our minds is where it differs. It's like death, it comes in many faces but it is still the same one thing that we all get to.

© Isabel K.T.

EUSTACE:
It is like death! (eureka moment) Fear and death, fear leads to death, to find death one must find fear.

The FOOL appears by EUSTACE mocking camaraderie as EUSTACE continues his thought process .

FOOL:
(in a whisper)
Are we still talking about the same thing?

EUSTACE:
(lost in thought)
Hmmm what?

FOOL:
Fear? Death?

EUSTACE:
Yes, we are. The same thing. (He pushes the Fool away from him) You aren't really funny did you know that?

FOOL:
Ah, but I am entertaining.

© Isabel K.T.

EUSTACE:
That is for me to say.

FOOL:
Would you prefer if I stood on my head making fun of the gossip I hear around town?

EUSTACE:
That sounds interesting.

FOOL:
Really? I thought perhaps you'd enjoy a conversation of more substance.

EUSTACE:
Never assume what I will or will not prefer.

FOOL:
Never.

EUSTACE:
What is the gossip?

FOOL:
They all talk about ghosts and hauntings.

© Isabel K.T.

EUSTACE:
You were right it, would have been more entertaining were you standing on your head.

FOOL stands on his head.

FOOL:
Like this?

EUSTACE:
Perhaps not. You may go now.

FOOL:
Yes, my lord.

FOOL leaves.

EUSTACE:
Useless entertainment. I wonder what my cousin does to entertain himself.

EUSTACE grabs another piece of chicken and continues eating.

© Isabel K.T.

(Scene IV)

Back at FORTINBRAS Castle on a late evening in the hall outside FORTINBRAS' study WESLEY is pacing as the GENERAL walks out.

GENERAL:
Ah Wesley, here still?

WESLEY:
General, just the person I was looking for.

GENERAL:
Why?

WESLEY:
Well I was thinking earlier today how little we know of each other. After all we do work together per se.

GENERAL:
And...?

WESLEY:
Well wouldn't it be nice if we were friends?

© Isabel K.T.

GENERAL:
I choose my friends Wesley.

WESLEY:
As do I, however, seeing that we both want what is best for Norway I really see no point in us bickering about.

GENERAL:
I wasn't aware we were bickering.

WESLEY:
Perhaps that is not the right word.

GENERAL:
Oh, then what is it?

WESLEY:
Perhaps we are misunderstanding each other. I hate misunderstandings, don't you?

GENERAL:
Why your sudden interest in cooperation? I was under the impression that all you cared for was favor from Lord Fortinbras.

© Isabel K.T.

WESLEY:
I do care for his favor, but I am an avid patriot as I have come to see are you.

GENERAL:
And why choose now to impose camaraderie?

WESLEY:
Well I had to be sure you and I were on the same page.

GENERAL:
I still don't think we are Wesley.

WESLEY:
But we are.

GENERAL:
Enlighten me.

WESLEY:
We both are trying to help Lord Fortinbras with his situation and establish peace around Norway are we not? I mean I know I am, and understand you want those same things too.

© Isabel K.T.

GENERAL:
I want what is best for Norway, but I believe we have different ideas of what that may be.

WESLEY:
How so?

GENERAL:
Wesley I have no time for a personal evaluation. I have important matters to attend to.

WESLEY:
Why are they so important to you General?

GENERAL:
Have we not gone through this already?

WESLEY:
Apparently not, for now I am not sure I understand where you are coming from seeing as you deny us having the same interests so please do enlighten me. I have done as much for you.

GENERAL:
You are giving me a headache.

© Isabel K.T.

WESLEY:
So sorry. Didn't think a man such as yourself would be so easily affected.

GENERAL:
I am not. But I didn't think a man such as yourself would be so concerned with friendships of any kind.

WESLEY:
Ah, that shows how little we know each other. My point exactly.

GENERAL:
What is it you want Wesley?

WESLEY:
You never did answer my question.

GENERAL:
Which is?

WESLEY:
Why are you so concerned with the situation?

© Isabel K.T.

GENERAL:
Why are you?

WESLEY:
Are you implying anything?

GENERAL:
Is there something to imply?

WESLEY:
I should think not. Yet you go and question me by denying our kinship.

GENERAL:
For a start, as you clearly have no respect on personal correspondence and privacy, I know we have very different ideas of the world. I don't need to know more.

WESLEY:
I'm going to pretend I didn't hear that. If you must know it is my duty to be sure that the letters arriving for our Lord are safe.

© Isabel K.T.

GENERAL:
What do you expect inside a letter, a wound-inflicting dagger, poison, death by paper cut?

WESLEY:
One can never be too careful.

GENERAL:
Very well then, you have your answer.

WESLEY:
So you stand by your way of the world?

GENERAL:
Anything you disapprove of Wesley?

WESLEY:
Oh, I'm sure a man such as you does not seek my approval.

GENERAL:
You are right. I do not. Now, let me pass.

© Isabel K.T.

WESLEY:
But I do wonder, how do you know your actions are patriotic?

GENRAL:
Excuse me?

WESLEY:
Yes, I'm having difficulty with this myself you see, and I was hoping you could help me out.

GENERAL:
How do you mean?

WESLEY:
Well, how do you know that your actions are patriotic? I understand how they can be loyal for they are loyal to Lord Fortinbras. However Lord Fortinbras is not the head of Norway, so how can loyalty to him be patriotic?

GENERAL:
Again Wesley, what are you trying to imply?

© Isabel K.T.

WESLEY:
Merely pointing out a situation that has been giving me grief for a while. I can't sleep well anymore you see.

GENREAL:
What a pity, you should try reading your own correspondence for a change.

WESLEY:
I don't know what to do.

GENERAL:
I cannot help you there Wesley. A man's sense of honor and loyalty are his own. I know my lord Fortinbras to be a Nordic patriot through and through, therefore by being loyal to him, I am indeed keeping my patriotism. I don't know what keeps you up at night. If you doubt Lord Fortinbras' loyalty to his people, then perhaps you shouldn't be advising him.

WESLEY:
You do not?

© Isabel K.T.

GENERAL:
No.

WESLEY:
Not even a tiny bit?

GENERAL:
No.

WESLEY:
Very well then you are in the clear.

GENERAL:
Excuse me?

WESLEY:
A little test you see. I wanted to be absolutely sure you were a loyalist. Things will get difficult and one needs to know where he and his fellow companions stand. Lord Fortinbras will need all the support he can get. It's good to know he has it. Perhaps we should get to know each other better.

© Isabel K.T.

GENERAL:
Well, I'm glad to hear this conversation will help you sleep at night. It does nothing for my sleep really.

WESLEY:
Why not? I hope I did not manage to have you questioning your patriotism now.

GENERAL:
Nothing of the sort. You may rest assured of my stance but I am far from assured of yours.

WESLEY:
You still doubt me?

GENERAL:
Of course.

WESLEY:
On what grounds?

GENERAL:
On the same grounds as before. You may have given me a test, but I have not given you one. You doubt me

© Isabel K.T.

and suggest me to doubt myself. So no, I do not have any incentive to trust you. I will leave now.

GENERAL leaves.

WESLEY:
This will prove harder than I thought. How can this man be so sure? Doesn't he see? Doesn't he worry he may be on the wrong side of things? How can he be so loyal to Fortinbras when there is also Eustace to consider on the race for the throne? What if he is wrong, what if Eustace wins and banishes or worst kills all of Fortibras' supporters? Can he not fear that? Perhaps he has none to fear for. He has never mentioned a family. Although I don't have one and yet I still fear this. What keeps him up at night? Surely the man has a weakness. I will have to pay closer attention. Follow him around perhaps? No, no he has a keen sense of awareness, I will only arise suspicion to myself. If only I were a bloody ghost. That would make things infinitely easier for me. Easily eavesdropping on everything. I would seldom make a mistake if I were always informed. Perhaps I could even clear my own doubts that way. I could follow Fortibras around, see

© Isabel K.T.

what he does... know his plans.... Now, wouldn't that be nice...

ABELINE walks by.

WESLEY:
Lady Fortinbras.

ABELINE:
Wesley. What are you doing around here at this time?

WESLEY:
I couldn't sleep my lady.

ABELINE:
Try warm milk.

WESLEY:
I will my lady.

ABELINE:
You are still here.

© Isabel K.T.

WESLEY:
I was trying to figure out this ghost nonsense. Thought perhaps if I walked the corridors I could see for myself if there is one in this castle.

ABELINE:
I was under the impression you didn't believe in ghosts, and understood the matter referred to a ghost elsewhere.

WESLEY:
Worry is contagious my lady.

ABELINE:
So it would seem. I would hurry to the kitchen if I were you. The servants may be speaking of your night walking by morning if they see you out and about without reason, and we all know how much you care for your image.

WESLEY:
Yes, I do. Thank you my lady.

ABELINE:
Good night Wesley.

© Isabel K.T.

ABELINE walks away, towards the office.

WESLEY:
The servants! Why didn't I think of that before? Surely someone knows something about the General. He must talk to someone besides Fortinbras. Or perhaps the servants have seen something worth knowing. After all they are everywhere and do like to gossip. And they are rarely noticed. I should become one myself! No, I wouldn't like waiting on others in such a fashion. I can still talk to them, be a little friendly. I'm sure they'll talk to whoever is willing to hear ha-ha! Poor things! That's it!

(Scene V)
ABELINE walks into the study.
FORTINBRAS is at his desk looking at charts and letters.

ABELINE:
What is going on?

© Isabel K.T.

FORTINBRAS:
Please do come in. What do you mean?

ABELINE:
Oh, come on Forti. It's not like you wouldn't let me walk in.

FORTINBRAS:
It's called protocol dear. How would you know I am not in a meeting?

ABELINE:
Right. Let me leave again.

FORTINBRAS:
No need now.

ABELINE:
Oh, I insist.

Turns and exits the office.

FORTINBRAS:
Come on Abbie, that's ridiculous.

© Isabel K.T.

ABELINE knocks.

ABELINE:
May I come in?

FORTINBRAS:
No.

ABELINE walks in.

ABELINE:
What?

FORTINBRAS:
See, you come in anyway.

ABELINE:
Fine. May I walk in further?

FORTINBRAS:
Please do.

ABELINE:
Hmmm.

© Isabel K.T.

FORTINBRAS:
What?

ABELINE:
I found Wesley pacing back and forth before I came here the first time and now I went out he was gone.

FORTINBRAS:
What was he doing out there?

ABELINE:
I don't know. I was hoping you could tell me. He seemed worried about something.

FORTINBRAS:
It's Wesley, he is always worried, it keeps him motivated.

ABELINE:
Said he couldn't sleep, so I told him to get some milk. He's probably down in the kitchens now. He was oddly amiable too.

© Isabel K.T.

FORTINBRAS:
That is strange. He was supposed to get back to me on something and he has not done so yet. If he had received bad news he would have been the first one to running in to tell them. He loves causing panic.

ABELINE:
I don't know what it was but he was bothered.

FORTINBRAS:
Perhaps he sleepwalks and we don't know.

ABELINE:
I didn't like it.

FORTINBRAS:
Abbie, if I worried about all you didn't like I'd live as worried as you all day. Please relax. We have an idea for this ghost situation and all is running smoothly with the General.

ABELINE:
He's a good man.

© Isabel K.T.

FORTINBRAS:
Yes, and a good friend.

ABELINE:
Good.

FORTINBRAS:
I don't think Wesley is what brought you over here tonight. What's going on?

ABELINE:
If I say I couldn't sleep would you believe me?

FORTINBRAS:
Yes, actually.

ABELINE:
I just had another bad dream.

FORTINBRAS:
Ah.

ABELINE:
I thought perhaps I could sit here with you, read something while you are done? I waited until

© Isabel K.T.

everyone had gone to bed. Wouldn't want to ruin your reputation.

FORTINBRAS:
Wesley was still out and about.

ABELINE:
Not much I could do there, your reputation with him is probably already ruined.

FORTINBRAS:
Probably.

ABELINE:
May I?

FORTINBRAS:
Yes, of course.

ABELINE:
Thank you.

FORTINBRAS:
Speaking of which how was everything with the Oracle.

© Isabel K.T.

ABELINE shrugs.

FORTINBRAS:
Abbie?

ABELINE:
Same old same old.

FORTINRBAS:
You could sleep couldn't you?
ABELINE:
Yes.

FORTINBRAS:
So why are you here?

ABELINE:
I thought perhaps you shouldn't be alone.

FORTINBRAS:
Abbie, please. I am a grown man, I can take care of myself.

© isabel K.T.

ABELINE:
I know. Still can you blame me for trying? I feel so useless.

FORTINBRAS:
I can assure you, you aren't.

ABELINE:
May I still stay?

FORTINBRAS:
Of course, just don't start with the ghost again.

ABELINE:
I have no idea what you are talking about.

(Scene VI)

WESLEY goes to the kitchens, there is noise and movement all over as servants are cleaning up. It is a stark contrast to the otherwise silent and empty looking rooms and hallways of the rest of the castle.

© Isabel K.T.

In the following scene a continuous shift in perspective takes place as he communicates with a young servant and the servant in turn communicates with the HEAD COOK. As WESLEY speaks all that comes out of his mouth, and all the HEAD COOK hears is gibberish and vice-versa. Gestures are used to further express the context of the expressions towards each other. A SERVANT who understands both, translates what each is saying. Those words are in ( ) under each character's gibberish dialogue.

WESLEY:
Evening.

Everyone stops mid-action.

COOK: Gibberish sound
(Evening. Wha' can we do for ya'?)

WESLEY: Gibberish sound
(I need a glass of warm milk.)

Cook bows, he turns to servant closest to him.

© Isabel K.T.

COOK: Gibberish sound
(Ya' 'eard him: Warm milk, 'urry.)

Other servants are quiet.

WESLEY looks at them.

Still quiet.

COOK:
(to other Servants)
Go back on to yer business.

WESLEY: Gibberish sound.
(Excuse me?)

COOK: Gibberish sound
(Not ya' sir, o'course. The lot' of'em.)

WESLEY: Gibberish sound
(Ah.)

Servant returns.

COOK: Gibberish sound

© Isabel K.T.

(Ah, 'ere we are. Is there anything else we can do fer ya' sir?)

WESLEY: Gibberish sound
(Actually, do any of you serve the General?)

COOK: Gibberish sound
(I cook eve'ry meal.)

SERVANT:
(to COOK)
He wants to know if we serve the General.

WESLEY: Gibberish sound
(I mean is there anyone here that serves the General personally?)

COOK: Gibberish sound
(No sir.)

WESLEY looks on, trying to find another way to continue the conversation. COOK thinks he did not understand his meaning this time.

© Isabel K.T.

COOK turns to SERVANT and motions for him to translate.

SERVANT:
(to Wesley)
No sir, no one here serves the General personally.

WESLEY: Gibberish sound
(Ah, I see. Well then nothing else.)

SERVANT:
(to Cook)
That was all.

COOK: Gibberish sound
(Goodnight sir.)

The COOK nods at WESLEY and is turning to leave when WESLEY sees another servant carrying a bushel of apples and gets an idea.

WESLEY: Gibberish sound.
(Wait, were you responsible for the apple tart this evening?)

© Isabel K.T.

SERVANT:
(to Cook)
He wants to know if you were responsible for the apple tart.

COOK: Gibberish sound
(Indeed, I was.)

WESLEY: Gibberish sound
(It was superb.)

WESLEY:
(turns to SERVANT)
Tell him, 'Well done,'

SERVANT:
(to Cook)
He enjoyed it. He says 'Well done'.

COOK: Gibberish sound
(Thank ya' sir.)

WESLEY: Gibberish sound
(I say, could you teach me?)

© Isabel K.T.

COOK looks at SERVANT.

SERVANT:
(To Wesley)
Teach ya' what sir?

WESLEY:
How to make it. The tart.

SERVANT:
(To Cook)
He wishes to learn how to make the tart.

COOK:
(To Servant)
O' course! Tell him.

SERVANT:
(mimicking Cook)
Of course!

WESLEY:
(to SERVANT)

© Isabel K.T.

Excellent. Not tonight of course. Perhaps in the evening, or early afternoon? When is the kitchen less crowded?

SERVANT:
Never, sir. It's mostly more crowded.

COOK looks sternly at SERVANT.

SERVANT:
(To Cook)
He wishes to know when the kitchen would be less crowded. I said it is mostly more crowded.

COOK:
Ah

WESLEY:
Ah.

COOK:
(To Servant)
But everyone eats lunch around fthree. So, there will be more space, tell him that.

© Isabel K.T.

SERVANT:
(to Wesley)
Around fthree would be a good time any day.

WESLEY: Gibberish sound
(Wonderful)

WESLEY:
(To Servant)
Just wonderful.

SERVANT:
(To Cook)
Wonderful.

COOK:
(To Servant)
All right. Is there Anything else?

SERVANT:
(To Wesley)
Is there anything else we can do fer ya sir?

© Isabel K.T.

WESLEY:
(To Servant)
Right, no, thank you.

WESLEY: Gibberish sound
(to Cook)
Thank you.

COOK bows, he nudges SERVANT to do the same.
WESLEY leaves.

SERVANT:
Funny fella isn't he?

COOK:
Yes, but with good taste.

SERVANT snorts. COOK turns to SERVANT.

COOK:
Get back to work.

© Isabel K.T.

(Scene VII)
Back at EUSTACE´s castle.

MESSENGER:
My Lord, this just came for you.

EUSTACE is busy eating a chicken. Motions his messenger to leave it at the table and leave. He looks at the letter and starts to choke. He gulps down his wine, cleans his hands on his clothes and opens the letter.

EUSTACE:
What does she want? It has to be her I'd recognize that handwriting anywhere.

He starts reading the letter.

EUSTACE:
Peace? Ha! I want what is rightfully mine. Why would she even dare mention this? After all these years...

He keeps reading.

© Isabel K.T.

EUSTACE:
She cannot do this! Who does she think she is! How will I answer her? If I acquiesce to her request then she will think I have yielded, given her some ultimate power to use against me at her whim. What if I say I wouldn't even if I already have? I need to speak with her. BOY get back here!

Messenger comes running in.

MESSENGER:
Yes, my lord.

EUSTACE:
Has the lady that delivered this left already?

MESSENGER:
There was no lady my lord.

EUSTACE:
Then who delivered this?

MESSENGER:
It was a messenger sir.

© Isabel K.T.

EUSTACE:
Of course, it would be.

MESSENGER:
Sir?

EUSTACE:
Never mind you. Can you catch that messenger? I have something for his mistress.

MESSENGER:
I´ll try, my lord.
EUSTACE:
Catch him!

MESSENGER:
Yes, sir—my lord.

Messenger runs.

EUSTACE gets a pen from his desk and writes in the back of the letter.

© Isabel K.T.

EUSTACE:

If you want to play games then do it in person my dear. If not, then just back off and keep your interest in embroidery.

© Isabel K.T.

ACT III

(Scene I)

Elsinore platform, same night. HORATIO and HAMLET await the appearance of the ghost.

HORATIO:
Look, my lord, it comes!

Enter GHOST.

HAMLET:
Angels and ministers of grace defend us!
Be thou a spirit of health or goblin damn'd,
Bring with thee airs from heaven or blasts from hell,
Be thy intents wicked or charitable,
Thou comest in such a questionable shape
That I will speak to thee. I'll call thee Hamlet,
King, father, royal Dane: O, answer me!
Let me not burst in ignorance, but tell
Why thy canonized bones, hearsed in death,

© Isabel K.T.

Have burst their cerements, why the sepulchre,
Wherein we saw thee quietly enurned,
Hath oped his ponderous and marble jaws,
To cast thee up again. What may this mean,
That thou, dead corse, again in complete steel,
Revisit'st thus the glimpses of the moon,
Making night hideous, and we fools of nature
So horridly to shake our disposition
With thoughts beyond the reaches of our souls?
Say, why is this? wherefore? what should we do?

GHOST beckons HAMLET and walks away.

HORATIO:
It beckons you to go away with it,
As if it some impartment did desire
To you alone.

MARCELLUS:
Look, with what courteous action
It waves you to a more removed ground.
But do not go with it.

HORATIO:
No, by no means.

© Isabel K.T.

HAMLET:
It will not speak. then I will follow it.

HORATIO:
Do not, my lord.

HAMLET:
Why, what should be the fear?
I do not set my life in a pin's fee
And for my soul, what can it do to that,
Being a thing immortal as itself?
It waves me forth again. I'll follow it.

HORATIO:
What if it tempt you toward the flood, my lord,
Or to the dreadful summit of the cliff
That beetles o'er his base into the sea,
And there assume some other horrible form,
Which might deprive your sovereignty of reason
And draw you into madness? think of it.
The very place puts toys of desperation,
Without more motive, into every brain
That looks so many fathoms to the sea
And hears it roar beneath.

© Isabel K.T.

GHOST re-appears and beacons him again.

ADLER to the side is getting ready to take his place. When GHOST re-appears and beacons HAMLET again, ADLER stops in his tracks and waits to the side, paying attention to what is happening.

HAMLET:
It waves me still. Go on; I'll follow thee.

MARCELLUS:
You shall not go, my lord.

HAMLET:
Hold off your hands.

HORATIO:
Be ruled. You shall not go.

HAMLET:
My fate cries out,
And makes each petty artery in this body
As hardy as the Nemean lion's nerve.
Still am I called. Unhand me, gentlemen.
By heav'n, I'll make a ghost of him that lets me!

© Isabel K.T.

I say, away! [to Ghost] Go on; I'll follow thee.

Exeunt GHOST and HAMLET.

HORATIO:
He waxes desperate with imagination.

MARCELLUS:
Let's follow. 'Tis not fit thus to obey him.

HORATIO:
Have after. To what issue will this come?

AGDAR arrives where ADLER is and startles him. AGDAR stops him from making any noise.

They both look on at what is going on on stage and then at each other puzzled.

MARCELLUS:
Something is rotten in the state of Denmark.

HORATIO:
Heaven will direct it.

© Isabel K.T.

MARCELLUS:
Nay, let's follow him.

Exeunt

ADLER and AGDAR motion to each other to be quiet and softly follow.

(Scene II)
Another part of the platform. We see HAMLET and the GHOST walking side by side. HORATIO and MARCELLUS follow far behind. Twins confused follows unnoticed from the sides.

Enter GHOST and HAMLET.

HAMLET:
Where wilt thou lead me? speak; I'll go no further.

GHOST:
Mark me.

© Isabel K.T.

HAMLET:
I will.

GHOST:
My hour is almost come,
When I to sulphurous and tormenting flames
Must render up myself.

HAMLET:
Alas, poor ghost!

GHOST:
Pity me not, but lend thy serious hearing
To what I shall unfold.

HAMLET:
Speak; I am bound to hear.

GHOST:
So art thou to revenge, when thou shalt hear.

HAMLET:
What?

© Isabel K.T.

GHOST:
I am thy father's spirit,
Doom'd for a certain term to walk the night,
And for the day confined to fast in fires
Till the foul crimes done in my days of nature
Are burnt and purged away. But that I am forbid
To tell the secrets of my prison-house
I could a tale unfold whose lightest word
Would harrow up thy soul, freeze thy young blood,
Make thy two eyes, like stars, start from their spheres,
Thy knotted and combined locks to part,
And each particular hair to stand on end
Like quills upon the fretful porpentine.
But this eternal blazon must not be
To ears of flesh and blood. List, list, O, list!
If thou didst ever thy dear father love—

HAMLET:
O God!

GHOST:
Revenge his foul and most unnatural murder.

HAMLET:
Murder!

© Isabel K.T.

GHOST:
Murder most foul, as in the best it is,
But this most foul, strange and unnatural.

HAMLET:
Haste me to know't, that I, with wings as swift
As meditation or the thoughts of love,
May sweep to my revenge.

GHOST:
I find thee apt;
And duller shouldst thou be than the fat weed
That roots itself in ease on Lethe wharf
Wouldst thou not stir in this. Now, Hamlet, hear.
'Tis given out that, sleeping in my orchard,
A serpent stung me. So the whole ear of Denmark
By a forged process of my death
Rankly abused: but know, thou noble youth,
The serpent that did sting thy father's life
Now wears his crown.

HAMLET:
O my prophetic soul! My uncle!

© Isabel K.T.

ADLER and AGDAR look on surprised.

A cat appears and ADLER jumps up. AGDAR prevents him from making any more noise by covering ADLER'S mouth.

AGDAR motions towards HAMLET and GHOST, telling ADLER through gestures not to distract them. AGDAR let's go of ADLER'S mouth and they turn in unison to look at the site before them, before turning to each other surprised.

GHOST:
Ay, that incestuous, that adulterate beast,
With witchcraft of his wit, with traitorous gifts—
O wicked wit and gifts, that have the power
So to seduce!— won to his shameful lust
The will of my most seeming-virtuous queen.
O Hamlet, what a falling-off was there!
From me, whose love was of that dignity
That it went hand in hand even with the vow
I made to her in marriage, and to decline
Upon a wretch whose natural gifts were poor

© Isabel K.T.

To those of mine!
But virtue, as it never will be moved,
Though lewdness court it in a shape of heaven,
So lust, though to a radiant angel link'd,
Will sate itself in a celestial bed,
And prey on garbage.
But soft, methinks I scent the morning air.
Brief let me be. Sleeping within my orchard,
My custom always of the afternoon,
Upon my secure hour thy uncle stole,
With juice of cursed hebenon in a vial,
And in the porches of my ears did pour
The leperous distilment, whose effect
Holds such an enmity with blood of man
That swift as quicksilver it courses through
The natural gates and alleys of the body,
And with a sudden vigour doth posset
And curd, like eager droppings into milk,
The thin and wholesome blood. So did it mine;
And a most instant tetter bark'd about,
Most lazar-like, with vile and loathsome crust,
All my smooth body.
Thus was I, sleeping, by a brother's hand,
Of life, of crown, of queen, at once dispatch'd,
Cut off even in the blossoms of my sin,

© Isabel K.T.

Unhousel'd, disappointed, unaneled,
No reckoning made, but sent to my account
With all my imperfections on my head.
O, horrible! O, horrible! most horrible!
If thou hast nature in thee, bear it not.
Let not the royal bed of Denmark be
A couch for luxury and damned incest.
But, howsoever thou pursuest this act,
Taint not thy mind, nor let thy soul contrive
Against thy mother aught: leave her to heaven,
And to those thorns that in her bosom lodge
To prick and sting her. Fare thee well at once.
The glow-worm shows the matin to be near,
And 'gins to pale his uneffectual fire.
Adieu, adieu! Hamlet, remember me.

Exit GHOST.

HAMLET:
O all you host of heaven! O earth! What else?
And shall I couple hell? O, fie! Hold, hold, my heart,
And you, my sinews, grow not instant old,
But bear me stiffly up. Remember thee?
Ay, thou poor ghost, while memory holds a seat
In this distracted globe. Remember thee?

© Isabel K.T.

Yea, from the table of my memory
I'll wipe away all trivial fond records,
All saws of books, all forms, all pressures past,
That youth and observation copied there,
And thy commandment all alone shall live
Within the book and volume of my brain
Unmix'd with baser matter: yes, by heaven.
O most pernicious woman!
O villain, villain, smiling, damned villain!
My tables,—meet it is I set it down,
That one may smile, and smile, and be a villain.
At least I'm sure it may be so in Denmark:
[He writes]
So, uncle, there you are. Now to my word:
It is 'Adieu, adieu! remember me.'
I have sworn 't.

MARCELLUS HORATIO:
[Within] My lord, my lord,--

MARCELLUS:
[Within] Lord Hamlet,--

HORATIO:
[Within] Heaven secure him!

© Isabel K.T.

HAMLET:
So be it!

HORATIO:
[Calling] Hillo, ho, ho, my lord!

HAMLET:
Hillo, ho, ho, boy! come, bird, come.

Enter HORATIO and MARCELLUS.

MARCELLUS:
How is't, my noble lord?

HORATIO:
What news, my lord?

HAMLET:
O, wonderful!

HORATIO:
Good my lord, tell it.

HAMLET:
No; you'll reveal it.

© Isabel K.T.

HORATIO:
Not I, my lord, by heaven.

MARCELLUS:
Nor I, my lord.

HAMLET:
How say you, then; would heart of man once think it?
But you'll be secret?

HORATIO MARCELLUS:
Ay, by heaven, my lord.

HAMLET:
There's ne'er a villain dwelling in all Denmark
But he's an arrant knave.

HORATIO:
There needs no ghost, my lord, come from the grave
To tell us this.

HAMLET:
Why, right; you are i' the right,
And so, without more circumstance at all
I hold it fit that we shake hands and part,

© Isabel K.T.

You, as your business and desire shall point you—
For every man has business and desire,
Such as it is— and for mine own poor part,
Look you, I'll go pray.

HORATIO:
These are but wild and whirling words, my lord.

HAMLET:
I'm sorry they offend you, heartily,
Yes, 'faith heartily.

HORATIO:
There's no offence, my lord.

HAMLET:
Yes, by Saint Patrick, but there is, Horatio,
And much offence too. Touching this vision here,
It is an honest ghost, that let me tell you.
For your desire to know what is between us,
O'ermaster 't as you may. And now, good friends,
As you are friends, scholars and soldiers, '
Give me one poor request.

© Isabel K.T.

HORATIO:
What is't, my lord? we will.

HAMLET:
Never make known what you have seen to-night.

HORATIO MARCELLUS:
My lord, we will not.

HAMLET:
Nay, but swear't.

HORATIO:
In faith, My lord, not I.

MARCELLUS:
Nor I, my lord, in faith.

HAMLET:
Upon my sword.

MARCELLUS:
We have sworn, my lord, already.

© Isabel K.T.

HAMLET:
Indeed, upon my sword, indeed.

Ghost:
[Beneath] Swear.

HAMLET:
Ah, ha, boy! say'st thou so? art thou there, truepenny?
Come on—you hear this fellow in the cellarage—
Consent to swear.

HORATIO:
Propose the oath, my lord.

HAMLET:
Never to speak of this that you have seen, Swear by my sword.

Ghost:
[Beneath] Swear.

HAMLET:
Hic et ubique? then we'll shift our ground.—
Come hither, gentlemen,
And lay your hands again upon my sword.

© Isabel K.T.

Never to speak of this that you have heard,
Swear by my sword.
Ghost:
[Beneath] Swear.

[They Swear]

HAMLET:
Well said, old mole! canst work i' the earth so fast?
A worthy pioneer— Once more remove, good friends.

HORATIO:
O day and night, but this is wondrous strange!

HAMLET:
And therefore as a stranger give it welcome.
There are more things in heaven and earth, Horatio,
Than are dreamt of in your philosophy. But come.
Here, as before, never, so help you mercy,
How strange or odd soe'er I bear myself—
As I perchance hereafter shall think meet
To put an antic disposition on—
That you, at such times seeing me, never shall,
With arms encumber'd thus, or this headshake,
Or by pronouncing of some doubtful phrase

© Isabel K.T.

As 'Well, well, we know,' or 'We could, an if we would,'
Or 'If we list to speak,' or 'There be, an if they might,'
Or such ambiguous giving out, to note
That you know aught of me— this not to do,
So grace and mercy at your most need help you,
swear.

Ghost:
[Beneath] Swear.

[They Swear]

HAMLET:
Rest, rest, perturbed spirit.—So, gentlemen,
With all my love I do commend me to you,
And what so poor a man as Hamlet is
May do to express his love and friending to you,
God willing, shall not lack. Let us go in together,
And still your fingers on your lips, I pray.
The time is out of joint: O cursed spite,
That ever I was born to set it right!
Nay, come, let's go together.

Exeunt.

© isabel K.T.

ADLER and AGDAR wait for a moment, then AGDAR walks confused onto the stage. He bends down to touch where the Ghost was, checking for any device.

ADLER walks in after him a finger on his lips to remind AGDAR to keep quiet. AGDAR nods. Their brume machine turns on, on its own. They look at each other in fear. Stage goes to black.

(Scene III)

Back in FORTINBRAS´ Castle, down in the busy kitchens. WESLEY is tying an apron on his waist.

WESLEY:
This is ridiculous.

SERVANT:
It's important sir.

WESLEY:
I do not need to be marked by this attire.

© Isabel K.T.

SERVANT:
Oh it's not for uniform purposeses.

WESLEY:
What is it for then?

COOK: Gibberish sound
(Move out of the way.)

COOK is making his way through the kitchen with a big pot filled with what looks like berry jam. He drops some on the floor.

COOK: Gibberish sound
(It's very 'ot and stains, so stay far away and let it do its business.)
WESLEY:
On second thought this is perfect. Do you have one for the top?

SERVANT:
You are funny.

© Isabel K.T.

WESLEY:
I beg your pardon?

SERVANT:
No need.

WESLEY:
I wasn't really asking for your pardon.

SERVANT:
Oh. Please speak clearly Sir. We have a lot of work ter do.

WESLEY:
Say does the General come down here often?

SERVANT:
I fthought you asked that last time.

WESLEY:
I did? My I must be really tired, can you believe I do not remember?

SERVANT:
No.

© Isabel K.T.

WESLEY:
I beg your pardon?

SERVANT:
You keep saying that. He sometimes comes down to thank us for the meals, or to pick up ther bones.

WESLEY:
Why would he do that?

SERVANT:
His dog.

WESLEY:
What dog?

SERVANT:
You don't know about his dog? It's a fierce one that one. I don't know the type but they don't make them like those anymore.

WESLEY:
So he gets bones for his dog.

© Isabel K.T.

SERVANT:
Oh yes, he gets only the bestest, the others we throw out. That dog is like a child to him.

WESLEY:
Really? How interesting?

SERVANT:
Nah, it happens with lonely people.

WESLEY:
You don't say.

SERVANT:
I do. The General is all alone see, so the only way he gets that human comfort is with 'is dog. I had an uncle like that.

WESLEY:
Company you mean?

SERVANT:
That too. Anyways he is very, very, very, close to this dog.

© Isabel K.T.

WESLEY:
And how do you know this?

SERVANT:
His dog got sick one time.

WESLEY:
And?

SERVANT:
He brought it with him. I took care of it myself.

WESLEY:
Ah.

SERVANT:
Real good at it too. I love dogs.

COOK:
(To Servant)
Witfh respect sir, are ya' two goi'n to cook or can ya' get aout? We 'ave a meal to prepare, all the room is needed.

Turns to WESLEY and nods.

© Isabel K.T.

WESLEY nods back.

SERVANT:
Sir, we better get on with the cooking.

WESLEY:
Actually, I think I'll come back some other time. Slight headache, you see.

SERVANT:
Oh, al'right. Just say so in advance.

WESLEY:
Charming.
WESLEY leaves.

(Scene IV)

Back at EUSTACE's Castle. EUSTACE is once more at the table, WESLEY walks in and bows.

EUSTACE:
Well? Did you find anything?

© Isabel K.T.

WESLEY:
I found something. It's not exactly useful.

EUSTACE:
Then don't waste my time.

EUSTACE motions him away.

WESLEY:
My Lord, it's all I could get. The General is clearer than the wind.

EUSTACE:
The wind is not even visible Wesley. Get to the point. What did you find?

WESLEY:
I found a dog.

EUSTACE:
A dog?

WESLEY:
Yes, well, the General has no family, no familial obligations, and his loyalty is absolute to Fortinbras.

© Isabel K.T.

As far as I can tell he has no weakness. He is a simple man, of duty and honor.

EUSTACE:
What about women? Does he show interest in women?

WESLEY:
No sir.

EUSTACE:
You may be onto something here Wesley.

WESLEY:
No particular woman rather, that would sway him away from his duty.

EUSTACE is disappointed.

EUSTACE:
So, a dog?

© Isabel K.T.

WESLEY:
Yes, sir. The dog is his whole family. He takes him with him everywhere and even has the kitchen save it bones.

EUSTACE:
What exactly do you propose we do with the General's dog Wesley?

WESLEY:
Well sir, I was thinking of taking it away.

EUSTACE:
And you consider that would be enough to weaken the General?

WESLEY:
Sir, it is my experience that all human beings seek comfort of some sort. Therefore, if we take away his one companion how will he find solace or company in his lonely nights?

EUSTACE:
We could try this.

© Isabel K.T.

WESLEY:
The dog is not easy to get to.

EUSTACE:
Wesley, it's a dog. Find a way.
WESLEY:
Yes, Sir.

WESLEY bows and leaves.

(Scene III)
Back at Fortinbras´ Castle. WESLEY goes down to the kitchens. Notes servant carrying a dog tray.

SERVANT:
Good to see ya' back sir.

WESLEY:
Yes, thank you. I say, where are you taking that?

© Isabel K.T.

SERVANT:
The General's dog sir. He's right outside and hasn't had his food yet you see.

COOK:
(to Servant)
Oi, come give mi a 'and with this.

SERVANT:
Ri'ght away.

WESLEY:
I could take the food.
SERVANT:
It wouldn't be proper'.

WESLEY:
If it weren't proper then would I even suggest it boy?

SERVANT:
No sir, you wouldn't sir.

WESLEY:
Good, then hand it over.

© Isabel K.T.

SERVANT:
Many thanks, sir.

SERVANT leaves to help COOK with the ingredients.

WESLEY:
This was too easy!

WESLEY goes to Dog Kennel, that suddenly appears on the farthest side of the stage.

WESLEY:
Here doggy doggy.

No Sound.

WESLEY:
Oh for Zeus´s sake. He kneels and crawls to the edge of the house dangling the plate in front of the doorway.

WESLEY gets pulled in, growling noises from the dog house.

© Isabel K.T.

(Scene IV)

FORTINBRAS is pacing in his study. ABELINE walks in.

ABELINE:
What´s wrong?

FORTINBRAS:
What do you mean?

ABELINE:
You are pacing.

FORTINBRAS:
Read.

ABELINE turns to the table where she sees an opened letter.

FORTINBRAS:
It is a summary of how the fields are doing. Apparently, we have been having a series of thefts. People are coming in and taking the farmer's crops in the middle of the night.

© Isabel K.T.

ABELINE:
Why hasn't something been done?

FORTINBRAS:
At the beginning they thought perhaps some wild animals were eating them but one of the farmers saw a couple of people last night with satchels full of his crops. He was unable to recognize or catch them.

ABELINE:
Then it's easy, all you have to do is raise security.

FORTINBRAS:
Not exactly, if I raise security it will weaken our march on Denmark and Poland.

ABELINE:
Can't other measures be taken?

FORTINBRAS:
We can't afford to shift much around at this point.

ABELINE:
Have you told the General about this?

© Isabel K.T.

FORTINBRAS:
He is on his way.

ABELINE:
I just came from the oracle.

FORTINBRAS:
Not now Abbie please. I have to fix this first.

ABELINE:
But—

GENERAL walks in.

GENERAL:
You called to see me, my lord?

FORTINBRAS:
Yes. We have a problem with the crops. Apparently, we are being robbed every night. What worries me is that an increase in security will weaken our numbers, not to mention how this affects our rations.

© Isabel K.T.

GENERAL:
Do we know how many men have been coming in at night?

FORTINBRAS:
They mention a couple, but these nights have been dark and I can assure you a couple cannot steal these significant amounts. My guess is that it is a couple from each angle at the same time. We would have to cover all our boarders.

GENERAL:
Or have lookouts at the rooftop of each tower preparing to fire whomever is out.

FORTINBRAS:
Yes, but we would have to make sure none of our people are out that late.

GENERAL:
I will get straight to it.

FORTINBRAS:
How many men would we need for the job?

© Isabel K.T.

GENERAL:
I would suggest two of our finest for each tower. They will get the job done swiftly.

FORTINBRAS:
That is at least fourteen.

GENERAL:
Yes, but infinitely less than having men around the whole perimeter.

FORTINBRAS:
Yes, yes. Very well then, make sure they are wearing their new armor for protection. We may as well make sure all is in order with it too before we end up like the French. (as an afterthought) And General, make sure the town knows they will need to be inside their homes by sundown.

ABELINE:
I am going to head down to the kitchens for some warm milk. Forti is there anything you might want?

FORTINBRAS:
I will come down with you dear. General?

© Isabel K.T.

GENERAL:
If I may, I'll join you both. I have to retrieve my dog from the kitchens.

FORTINBRAS:
Of course. Let's continue this conversation later. It would be unwise to discuss matters further on the way.

ABELINE:
Are you afraid of ghosts now darling?

FORTINBRAS:
Walls have better ears than ghosts my dear.

(Scene V)

In the empty kitchen. ABELINE, FORTINBRAS, and the GENERAL walk into the kitchen. ABELINE turns on the light.

ABELINE:
I will go get the milk.

© Isabel K.T.

FORTINBRAS:
Very well then.

GENERAL walks through to the end and goes for his dog. FORTINBRAS sits down at the table thinking.

(Scene VI)
GENERAL goes to the dog kennel. He keeps calling out for his dog, Thyre.

GENREAL:
Here Thyre, come here boy!
Silence

GENERAL:
That's strange.

GENERAL sticks his head into the dog kennel.

GENERAL:
By Juno! Let him go!

© Isabel K.T.

GENERAL drags a disheveled WESLEY out of the dog kennel.

ABELINE and FORTINBRAS hear the commotion and head over towards the dog kennel. FORTINBRAS stands in front of ABELINE protectively.

FORTINBRAS:
What's this?

GENERAL walks into the kitchen half carrying a disheveled WESLEY.

GENERAL:
I just found Wesley inside the dog house. Who knows how long he's been in there for.

ABELINE moves past FORTINBRAS.

ABELINE:
Let me take a look.

GENERAL sits WESLEY down on a small stool.

© Isabel K.T.

FORTINBRAS:
What were you doing down there Wesley?

WESLEY is in a state, talking gibberish. ABELINE rushes to get a bottle of alcohol and some clothes. She comes back with all in hand.

WESLEY:
(Gibberish)
houemsno skoirne

ABELINE:
Give him some room. I'll get him back to you in no time.

FORTINRBAS:
Come General, let's continue our discussion. I have some thoughts about the missing rations.

FORTINBRAS and GENERAL leave.

ABELINE tends to WESLEY's wounds.

ABELINE:
Fine mess you made of yourself Wesley.

© Isabel K.T.

WESLEY:
(he winces)
Never again. I don't care what he wants. Never again.

ABELINE:
Who wants?

WESLEY:
Oh sure, a dog, just a DOG!

ABELINE:
What are you talking about Wesley?

WESLEY:
The dog!

ABELINE:
Yes, the dog.

WESLEY:
I didn't get it. (pause) I – didn't – get – the DOG!

ABELINE:
Get the dog for whom?

© Isabel K.T.

WESLEY:
Aren't you paying attention?

ABELINE:
The man that robed the crops?

WESLEY:
Who robbed what?

ABELINE:
Never mind, tell me more about this dog.

WESLEY:
It's a menace, an absolute menace! I don't care if it helps. No. No. NOO. Dogs.

ABELINE:
Ok, Wesley no dogs. Now stay still.

ABELINE pouring alcohol on WESLEYS wounds as he tries in vain not to cry out in pain and twist away from her attempts.

© Isabel K.T.

(Scene VII)

Back at Fortinbras Castle. Fortinbras walks lost in thought towards his bedroom. In the bedroom ABELINE sits by the fireplace and thinks over the chess set with the game half-played. FORTINBRAS walks in.

ABELINE:
What happened dear? Any news on the thieves.

FORTINBRAS:
None yet, the guards are on a look out but we are sure they will come.

ABELINE:
I wish they wouldn't.

FORTINBRAS:
We all do.

ABELINE looks down at the Chess board.

© Isabel K.T.

ABELINE:
You know, if a Queen actually had as much leeway on the floor as she has on the board, she would keep everything in shape.

FORTINBRAS:
... and the King would be pretty much useless?

ABELINE:
Not useless, focused on other things. Each role in the game has a part to play.

FORTINBRAS:
Even a ghost?

ABELINE:
(sighs) Even, yes. Although right now I envy the ghost's omnipresent freedom to move about and do, it's almost like this Queen's. (she grabs the Queen chess piece)

FORTINBRAS sits next to her and looks at the game.

ABELINE:
What will happen next Forti?

© Isabel K.T.

FORTINBRAS:
What do you mean? (looking at the board) You still haven't moved.

ABELINE:
I mean what's next. Are you making a move on Denmark?

FORTINBRAS:
I have to be sure things here are alright first. I cannot leave the country and leave you here while there is so much to sort out.

ABELINE:
I can manage our land.

FORTINBRAS:
I know you can, but how could I leave to conquer land for my country, when I am neglecting the land in my country?

ABELINE:
Is it really that bad?

© Isabel K.T.

FORTINBRAS:
The General and I have been talking. It seems like the crops have been a ruse to start causing fights between our tenants.

ABELINE:
What for?

FORTINBRAS:
Someone clearly wants to cause havoc and I think I know who it is.

ABELINE:
Eustace!

FORTINBRAS:
Who else?

ABELINE:
I think you should question Wesley once he recovers. He kept mumbling about being sent for the dog and never again working for "him." Whomever "him" is, I am pretty sure he would know the answer to your question. Besides he has always been a little git and

© Isabel K.T.

would be the one to play two sides. You always knew this.

FORTINBRAS:
Hmm...Yes, true, but he doesn't know much of our plan of action.

ABELINE:
You are too distracted. There is something else.

FORTINBRAS:
My uncle has summoned me to his chambers first thing tomorrow morning.

ABELINE:
Did he say what for?

FORTINBRAS:
Only that it is imperative I am there at his feet by the rooster's crow.

ABELINE:
Let's get some sleep then. You will be all the better for having some rest.

© Isabel K.T.

ABELINE stands up and gives out her hand for FORTINBRAS to take. He takes it. They walk towards the bed. The light dims out.

(Scene VIII)

ABELINE & FORTINBRAS' bedroom. They sleep soundly when ABELINE wakes up with an idea. She kisses FORTINBRAS and quietly exits the bed.

(Scene IX)

ABELINE walks along a dimly lit corridor with a candle in her hand and knocks on the door. A woman in her nightgown opens the door. ABELINE motions to be quiet and walks inside. The woman closes behind her.

(Scene X)

ABELINE returns to her bedroom with FORTINBRAS. She blows out the candle and quietly gets back in bed.

© Isabel K.T.

FORTINBRAS:
Is everything alright sweetheart?

ABELINE:
Yes, darling, everything is alright.

She kisses him and holds him in her arms.

(Scene XI)

The following sequence happens in silence. While the characters move to their respective spaces, we see all played out on stage. We see the door ABELINE knocked on earlier in the night open. Four women walk out, the last one is fixing her clothes as they disperse through the stage to different areas of the CASTLE. The scene (or scenes) progress with the sun coming slowly out.

The first woman goes to speak to the archer at the top of the castle. She explains something and stands guard by him.

The second woman goes to the village and finds the point of intersection in the road between two of the crop

© Isabel K.T.

fields that are being disturbed. She falls to the ground there.

The third woman goes to the castle guards at the base of the castle and proceeds to flirtingly start a conversation.

The fourth woman goes down to the kitchens and opens the stock room and starts inspecting and counting the provisions there.

Whenever the respective characters find the truth, or succeed in their task, the light expands in the frame and they leave the frame to find the others.

The first one to finish her task is the fourth woman in the kitchen. She finds a discrepancy in the count, the light shines on the frame and she excitedly exits the room.

The second one to finish her task is the third woman, as she gets the information she needs from her conversation with the guards the light comes on in the frame and she leaves.

The third one to finish her task is the second woman, as a group of strangers accidentally trip over her leg and help

© Isabel K.T.

her out. A cabbage rolls out of the satchel as she looks up at his face under the hood, the light shines on the frame. As she thanks the gentleman for his assistance, she hooks a small pocket mirror to his cloak. Light comes back on the frame as they go their separate ways.

The fourth one to finish her task, is the first woman. Finding the reflection of the mirror she shows the archer where to aim and shots are fired. The light comes to the frame, and the woman leaves it just as the thieves are surrounded and caught by the guards below.

(Scene XII)

A knock at ABELINE's bedroom door. She opens. One of the ladies is at her door. All we hear is a whisper as she is given four parchment notes. The lady says a single word for each note as she turns over the parchments to her: Who, Where, Why, & How.

The rooster crows ... it's morning.

© Isabel K.T.

(Scene XIII)

Uncle's bedroom. Early morning. FORTINBRAS' Uncle is in bed, furious. Next to him stands EUSTACE trying and failing to hide his glee.

FORTINBRAS walks in, unsurprised at seeing EUSTACE there.

FORTINBRAS:
Good morning Uncle.

UNCLE:
What is it I hear of you and Denmark?

FORTINBRAS:
What about me and Denmark?

UNCLE:
Don't play coy with me boy! I know. I received an angry letter from King Claudius.

EUSTACE is having a hard time containing his enjoyment.

FORTINBRAS remains silent.

© Isabel K.T.

UNCLE:
Perhaps I did not make myself clear before, under no circumstance, in any way or form, are you to interfere with Denmark. Is that understood?
FORTINBRAS:
Yes. I will not interfere with Denmark, but you see Uncle I am afraid King Claudius is somewhat misinformed, I only need passage through Denmark. My attention is directed towards Poland now. Would you have any objections to that?

EUSTACE:
Uncle it's a ruse. He is just trying to frame you to take the crown.

UNCLE:
Silence! What did I do to deserve this? One will not understand the meaning of diplomacy and the other, the other has the emotional intelligence of a two-year-old soup.

UNCLE ponders for a moment.

UNCLE:

© Isabel K.T.

Very well Fortinbras, I will write to Claudius to ask permission for your crossing, but let me make myself perfectly clear, I will also give him full permission to dispose of you and any person loyal to you if you for one minute disobey my command. If you attack Denmark it is entirely on your own and Norway will forever wash it's hands of you.

FORTINBRAS:
I understand Uncle. Thank you.
UNCLE:
Good. You may go now. Wait for my instructions on when to leave and I want a copy of the road you plan to take.

FORTINBRAS:
It will be in your hands by tomorrow.

FORTINBRAS nods, bows, and steals a glance at EUSTACE before he exits the room.

EUSTACE:
Well done Uncle! That showed him. Who does he thing he is besmirching our name-?

© Isabel K.T.

UNCLE:
Oh, do shut up! The only reason you are in line for the throne is because you are blood. You are a default not a choice. Just leave.

EUSTACE:
(in a whisper) It still gets me what I want.

EUSTACE leaves enjoying the moment.

(Scene XIV)

FORTINBRAS' study, everything is as he last left it.

FORTINBRAS walks in in a fury.

FORTINBRAS:
YOU! (pointing at the painting of his father) This is all on you! What were you thinking? No, wait, did you ever stop to think or were you just trying to prove yourself? Rushing into foolish acts to prove what? Your honor? Your nobility? Your courage? Ha! You had everything and threw it all away in a game of chance, and you call that honor? Why? Why did you prepare

© Isabel K.T.

me for a life of king? What was he point of it all when you were leaving your crown to your brother? Was this my punishment or yours to see this country cower away? And who is next, cousin Eustace? (he laughs because he doesn't want to cry) You are my own personal ghost; a haunting I can't seem to be rid off. Not anymore. Whatever I do from here on out is about me and my life. You hear me? Enough of you and what you wanted, enough of your legacy. I don't like the legacy you chose. Your legacy ended with you, and that's on you. It's about me this time. My time to do things my way.

FORTINBRAS goes up to the portrait and violently un-hangs it. He catches his breath.

ABELINE walks in, she notices the situation, gently approaches FORTINBRAS who is still holding the painting. She helps him loosen his grip on the painting, puts it to one side, and hugs him. They stand in silence for a spell.

ABELINE:
I like what you did with the room.

© Isabel K.T.

FORTINBRAS laughs.

ABELINE takes a letter from her pocket.

ABELINE:
A letter came for you.

FORTINBRAS:
Another ghost.

ABELINE:
Is it about the ghost?

FORTINBRAS puts the letter aside without opening it.

FORTINBRAS:
It doesn't matter now sweetheart, we are not taking Denmark, only passing through.

ABELINE:
Good.

FORTINBRAS:
You aren't going to ask me about my meeting?
ABELINE:

© Isabel K.T.

Only if you want to tell me.

FORTINBRAS:
I have to speak to the General. We need to seize the haunting and change our course. Denmark must see us coming if they are to trust we are only crossing the road to get to Poland.

ABELINE:
Can you trust Claudius to keep his word?

FORTINBRAS:
To my uncle yes, he wouldn't want to incur his wrath. Besides, why harm us when we are on our way to battle? If he believes in our success, he will want to keep the peace to make further treaties with my uncle; and if he doesn't, then he will have someone else get rid of the threat for him. (pause) We will prepare ourselves nevertheless.

ABELINE nods.

ABELINE:
You go do what you need to do, I'll manage here. Besides, we caught the crop stealers.

© Isabel K.T.

FORTINBRAS:
How?

ABELINE:
It's not important now. I figured out what the Queen can do.

FORTINBRAS:
Yes, you did. Thank you.

ABELINE:
Always. When do you leave?

FORTINBRAS:
When my uncle tells me. I would expect in a fortnight or two.

ABELINE:
Good. I get to have you for myself a little longer.

FORTINBRAS:
Abbie, darling, didn't you hear me? There is no more ghost.

© Isabel K.T.

ABELINE looks intently at him for a moment.

ABELINE:
You know, for the first time, I believe you.

© isabel K.T.

ACT IV

(Scene I)

FORTINBRAS and his army arrive at a plain in Denmark.

Enter FORTINBRAS, a Captain, and Soldiers, marching behind.

PRINCE FORTINBRAS:
Go, captain, from me greet the Danish king;
Tell him that, by his license, Fortinbras
Craves the conveyance of a promised march
Over his kingdom. You know the rendezvous.
If that his majesty would aught with us,
we shall express our duty in his eye;
And let him know so.

CAPTAIN:
I will do't, my lord.

PRINCE FORTINBRAS:
Go softly on.

© Isabel K.T.

Exeunt FORTINBRAS and Soldiers.

Enter from opposite side HAMLET, ROSENCRATZ, GUIDENSTERN,and others.

HAMLET:
Good sir, whose powers are these?

CAPTAIN:
They are of Norway, sir.

HAMLET:
How purposed, sir, I pray you?

CAPTAIN:
Against some part of Poland.

HAMLET:
Who commands them, sir?

CAPTAIN:
The nephew to old Norway, Fortinbras.

HAMLET:

© Isabel K.T.

Goes it against the main of Poland, sir, or for some frontier?

CAPTAIN:
Truly to speak, and with no addition,
We go to gain a little patch of ground
That hath in it no profit but the name.
To pay five ducats, five, I would not farm it;
Nor will it yield to Norway or the Pole
a ranker rate, should it be sold in fee.
HAMLET:
Why, then the Polack never will defend it.

CAPTAIN:
Yes, it is already garrison'd.

HAMLET:
Two thousand souls and twenty thousand ducats
Will not debate the question of this straw.
This is the imposthume of much wealth and peace,
That inward breaks, and shows no cause without
Why the man dies. I humbly thank you, sir.

CAPTAIN:
God be wi' you, sir.

© Isabel K.T.

Exit Captain.

HAMLET looks around.

FORTINBRAS walks on stage, his GENERAL and soldiers behind him. As they cross, FORTINBRAS and HAMLET are parallel to each other for a brief moment.

They look at each other in passing and nod before they continue walking in opposite directions.

Before exiting, FORTINBRAS turns to look behind him at HAMLET before he exits.

As HAMLET exits FORTINBRAS turns to the GENERAL who is now by his side.

FORTINBRAS:
General, did the Captain say where is Hamlet going?

GENERAL:
To England.

All exit.

© Isabel K.T.

(Scene II)

Back at EUSTACE Castle. Day. EUSTACE is having his usual feast of chicken.

SERVANT:
A letter for you my lord.

EUSTACE:
Leave it here.

SERVANT:
Yes, my lord.

Servant leaves.

EUSTACE:
Let's see Denmark... (he opens the letter) Why didn't I think of that? What a brilliant idea! Poland HA! Oh cousin of mine you make things so easy for me. I shall drink to you dear cousin and your soon demise.

EUSTACE drinks from his cup and sees it is empty, he continues to eat his chicken leg.

© Isabel K.T.

EUSTACE:
Boy! More wine!

He starts writing a note as he chews and laughs. He starts coughing, choking, and suddenly falls flat on the table. A Servant hears the thud and rushes in.

SERVANT:
My lord!

Servant moves EUSTACE.

SERVANT:
Help!

BERGDORF rushes over.

BERGDORF:
What happened?

SERVANT:
He was reading a letter. I heard laughing, and coughing, and that was that. I was outside. Heard a thump and came running.

© Isabel K.T.

BERGDORF:
What did you put in that cup?

Servant looks at the cup.

SERVANT:
It wasn't the cup, he was eating chicken. My cousin died of that once.

BERGDORF:
Death by chicken?

SERVANT:
The small bones, if not chewed properly, they can choke you.

BERGDORF:
What? You chew the bones?

SERVANT:
You don't?

BERGDORF:
No.

© Isabel K.T.

SERVANT:
We could look.

BERGDORF:
At what?

SERVANT:
His throat.

BERGDORF:
Do you know how to look at that?

SERVANT:
I reckon so.

BERGDORF opens EUSTACE's mouth as the Servant looks in.

SERVANT:
It's a bone alright. There's no room for light further down.

BERGDORF:
We have to call a physician.

© isabel K.T.

Servant checks for a heartbeat.

SERVANT:
It is too late. The pulse is gone.

BERGDORF closes his eyes and lowers his head.

BERGDORF:
May he rest in peace.

Servant bows his head.

(Scene III)
ABELINE is in her parlor reading a book.
In the parlor is a seating set, a table, and a fireplace.

Servant walks in.

SERVANT:
A message for you my lady.

© Isabel K.T.

He hands her a letter.

ABELINE:
Thank you.

Servant leaves.

ABELINE opens the letter.

ABELINE:
He is dead? A piece of chicken? Now, really.

ABELINE places the letter to the side and continues with her book.

Another servant walks in.

SERVANT:
There is a message for you my lady.

Servant hands over the second letter.

ABELINE is surprised.

ABELINE:

© Isabel K.T.

Thank you.

Servant leaves.

ABELINE opens the letter and reads it in hushed tones.

THE LETTER:
"Before the deed was done, fate intervened."

ABELINE:
How about that! (surprised) Eustace, you always were quite cannibalistic. Oh, what a relief! (sighs and relaxes)

She throws the second letter to the fire.

(Scene IV)

Drums of battle sound from far away, softly fading in. FORTINBRAS arrives in Denmark victorious from Poland as HAMLET lays slain on HORATIO'S arms. Scene opens where HAMLET ends, at the end of the match.

© Isabel K.T.

HAMLET:
As thou'rt a man,
Give me the cup. Let go. By heaven, I'll ha't.
O good Horatio, what a wounded name,
Things standing thus unknown, shall live behind me!
If thou didst ever hold me in thy heart,
Absent thee from felicity awhile,
And in this harsh world draw thy breath in pain
To tell my story.
March afar off, and shot within
What warlike noise is this?

OSRIC:
Young Fortinbras, with conquest come from Poland,
To the ambassadors of England gives
This warlike volley.

HAMLET:
O, I die, Horatio!
The potent poison quite o'er-crows my spirit.
I cannot live to hear the news from England,
But I do prophesy the election lights
On Fortinbras: he has my dying voice.
So tell him, with the occurrents, more and less,
Which have solicited. The rest is silence.

© Isabel K.T.

O,O,O,O!

HAMLET Dies.

HORATIO:
Now cracks a noble heart.
Good night sweet prince:
And flights of angels sing thee to thy rest.—
Why does the drum come hither?

Enter FORTINBRAS, the English Ambassadors, and others.

PRINCE FORTINBRAS:
Where is this sight?

HORATIO:
What is it ye would see?
If aught of woe or wonder, cease your search.

PRINCE FORTINBRAS:
This quarry cries on havoc. O proud death,
What feast is toward in thine eternal cell
That thou so many princes at a shot
So bloodily hast struck!

© Isabel K.T.

FIRST AMBASSADOR:
The sight is dismal,
And our affairs from England come too late.
The ears are senseless that should give us hearing
To tell him his commandment is fulfilled,
That Rosencrantz and Guildenstern are dead.
Where should we have our thanks?

HORATIO:
Not from his mouth,
Had it the ability of life to thank you.
He never gave commandment for their death.
But since, so jump upon this bloody question
You from the Polack wars, and you from England,
Are here arrived give order that these bodies
High on a stage be placed to the view;
And let me speak to the yet unknowing world
How these things came about: so shall you hear
Of carnal, bloody, and unnatural acts,
Of accidental judgments, casual slaughters,
Of deaths put on by cunning and forced cause;
And, in this upshot, purposes mistook
Fall'n on the inventors' reads. All this can I
Truly deliver.

© Isabel K.T.

PRINCE FORTINBRAS:
Let us haste to hear it,
And call the noblest to the audience.
For me, with sorrow I embrace my fortune.
I have some rights of memory in this kingdom,
Which now to claim my vantage doth invite me.

HORATIO:
Of that I shall have also cause to speak,
And from his mouth whose voice will draw on more.
But let this same be presently performed,
Even while men's minds are wild; lest more mischance
On plots and errors, happen.

PRINCE FORTINBRAS:
Let four captains
Bear Hamlet, like a soldier, to the stage,
For he was likely, had he been put on,
To have proved most royally: and, for his passage,
The soldiers' music and the rites of war
Speak loudly for him.Take up the bodies: such a sight
as this Becomes the field, but here shows much amiss.
Go, bid the soldiers shoot.

© Isabel K.T.

A dead march. Exeunt, bearing off the dead bodies; after which a peal of ordnance is shot off.

(Scene V)

FORTINBRAS is walking in the halls of Elsinore. The GENERAL catches up with him.

GENERAL:
My lord. A letter arrived.

FORTINBRAS turns around.

GENERAL:
From Lady Fortinbras.

The GENERAL hands him a letter.

FORTINBRAS reads the letter and looks up.

FORTINBRAS:
Eustace is dead, my Uncle is soon to join him it seems.

© Isabel K.T.

GENERAL:
I'm sorry my lord.

FORTINBRAS:
Thank you. (pauses, taking it all in) So much unnecessary death.

GENERAL:
(the General knows who he is talking about)
He was a haunted man.

FORTINBRAS:
I believe we had something to do with that.

GENERAL:
From what I hear my lord, our twins experienced the haunting themselves as much as they gave it. He was a good man, a smart man, his situation most unfortunate.

FORTINBRAS:
I think all ghosts have finally been laid to rest now. (pause) How are things coming along?

© Isabel K.T.

GENERAL:
They are coming along.

FORTINBRAS:
Good. I will be with you shortly.

GENERAL leaves a pensive FORTINBRAS.

FORTINBRAS looks at the letter in his hand and exits.

(Scene VI)
ROAYL DANISH graveyard. FORTINBRAS visits HAMLET's grave.

FORTINBRAS stands before HAMLET's grave. He remains silent for a moment.

FORTINBRAS:
Here we are after all this. I did not understand how much you and I shared a likeness. Our fathers were fools who left in their death more duty than what they gave us in life. A most unnecessary haunting that

© Isabel K.T.

invaded our actions, our thoughts, our peace. I salute your earnestness in finding truth amongst liars. Had I known you, perhaps we could have helped each other get rid of the usurpers of power who once laying in the shadows took our birthright in broad daylight. So much for so little, they never understood the price. They cannot hold onto what was never theirs, that is the death they know in life. Their haunting. For us, what is death if not another opportunity to live? A reminder of beauty not yet lost. Your story will not fade young prince. For my part, I am sorry I did not know you sooner. I will not let any more death overshadow life. From this moment on, it will seize to be anything other than a reminder of all that is precious and all there is yet to live for; and there is so much yet to live for. So much to love. I have been blessed with both great love and great friendship, things that are easy to overlook in their simplicity, yet they are deep in their richness. That you find both is my wish to you wherever you are. (pause) I will bring glory back to Denmark, just as I will do to Norway. This is my promise to you. Sleep well, the ghosts have been laid to rest.

© Isabel K.T.

FORTINBRAS touches the tombstone and looks up at the horizon for a moment, the sun is rising.

He exits. The sun rises.

The lights slowly and gradually fade to BLACKOUT.

THE END.

© Isabel K.T.

Hi! Here's something you may want to know about the story you just read. "Fortinbras, Prince of Norway" is inspired by character's in William Shakespeare's "Hamlet, Prince of Denmark," as well as techniques, stylings, and character presentations William Shakespeare used in other plays. This play follows the unseen journey of Fortinbras while in Norway, and uses pieces of "Hamlet, Prince of Denmark" to establish the journey in the same storyline as "Hamlet." The concept has been to explore how Fortinbras — who was in a very similar situation to Hamlet— found a different way forward for himself, and the elements that aided in that trajectory. If you are a fan of William Shakespeare or just a curious reader, I hope you enjoy these characters and this story. It has brought me great joy to write it.

First published in the United States of America on 2025 by Calelei™ Productions.

Copyright © 2025 Isabel K. T.
All rights reserved.

This publication may not be reproduced, stored, or used in any manner whatsoever — in part or whole — without written permission of the copyright owner.

Calelei™ Productions values and supports copyright. Thank you for respecting this copyright and purchasing an authorized edition of this book. Copyright encourages free expression, kindles creativity, and promotes artistic works, enriching culture. We appreciate your cooperation in not reproducing, scanning, distributing, storing, or supporting the unauthorized reproduction, scanning, storage, or distribution of this book or any of its parts. Your respect supports our creativity and we are grateful for it.

If you would like to use any material from this book please contact us at hello@caleleiproductions.com

ISBN: 978-1-7363180-9-6
eISBN: 978-1-7363180-8-9

Library of Congress Control Number: 2025906501

ABOUT THIS BOOK:
"Fortinbras, Prince of Norway" By Isabel K.T.
First Edition, March 2025 I First Print, March 2025 I English Language
The fonts used in this book were "Elsie Swash Caps" for the cover and title, as well as "Encode Sans" for the dialogue (regular) and scenes (thin). "Open Sans" for all other text. Cover art by Nicorene Stassen. Cover design by Isabel K.T.

Please note that the publisher is not responsible for any other website (or content) other than the publishers'. Visit us anytime:

Calelei™ Productions
www.caleleiproductions.com

We love Trees. Follow our tree planting at caleleiproductions.com/trees

"TO POSSIBILITY & TO THE LOVE THAT THRIVES IN IT.
TO LOVE & FRIENDSHIP."

(To my Love, my family, & my friends. Thank You <3.)

© Isabel K.T.